Building Dynamic Web Experiences with PHP

Harness the power of PHP to build dynamic and scalable websites

Dr. Surabhi Shanker

www.bpbonline.com

FIRST EDITION 2024

ISBN: 978-93-55516-596

Distributors:

BPB PUBLICATIONS
20, Ansari Road, Darya Ganj
New Delhi-110002
Ph: 23254990/23254991

DECCAN AGENCIES
4-3-329, Bank Street,
Hyderabad-500195
Ph: 24756967/24756400

MICRO MEDIA
Shop No. 5, Mahendra Chambers,
150 DN Rd. Next to Capital Cinema,
V.T. (C.S.T.) Station, MUMBAI-400 001
Ph: 22078296/22078297

To View Complete BPB Publications Catalogue Scan the QR Code:

Published by Manish Jain for BPB Publications, 20 Ansari Road, Darya Ganj, New Delhi-110002 and Printed by him at Manipal Technologies, Manipal

www.bpbonline.com

Dedicated to

In loving memory of my Mother-in-law, whose love continues to inspire us. With gratitude for her blessings and the enduring impact she had on our lives.

About the Author

Dr. Surabhi Shanker has accomplished her Ph.D. in the field of Semantic Web. With a Ph.D. in hand since 2016, she has 15 years of experience teaching UG and PG level students at different universities and affiliated colleges. She is a prolific researcher, and has authored and co-authored several impactful papers on topics ranging from Blockchain technology to AI & ML and E-Commerce. Her work has been featured in reputed journals and conferences. She has also authored various books, patents and chapters to various publications. Dr. Shanker's dedication to advancing knowledge in the Tech World is evident through her extensive academic and research contributions. She is passionate about sharing knowledge and has actively contributed to the PHP community through writing engagements. She aims to empower developers to excel in PHP and achieve excellence in web development.

About the Reviewer

Dr. Saloni Bhushan is a highly esteemed academician with a wealth of knowledge and expertise in the field of computer science. With an illustrious career spanning more than two decades, Dr. Bhushan has made significant contributions to the field through a seamless combination of teaching, research, and academic leadership.

She started her professional career in 1999 as a trainer in the computer field. She then, shifted to software development and worked as a programmer in a private limited company. After gaining practical knowledge and successfully completing several projects, her zeal and enthusiasm for teaching brought her back into full-time academics in the year 2007. She, then, embarked on her academic journey with a passion for fostering intellectual curiosity and academic excellence. She earned her doctoral degree from BRABU. Throughout her career, Dr. Bhushan has been dedicated to imparting knowledge to generations of students.

In addition to her exemplary teaching career, Dr. Bhushan is a prolific researcher. Her research has been published in reputed national and international conferences and international journals. She has also authored various book chapters.

Dr. Bhushan has also played a pivotal role in academic leadership, having served as a Department Head. Beyond the academic realm, Dr. Bhushan is an active member of professional societies and continues to contribute to the academic community through her involvement in editorial roles, conference organizing committees, etc.

Acknowledgement

Firstly, I would like to express my gratitude to almighty God for his blessings. I am immensely thankful to my family and friends for their unwavering support and encouragement throughout the process of writing this book, with a special mention to my husband, Amit, and my kids.

Additionally, I extend my appreciation to the management of K.R. Mangalam University for their consistent encouragement and guidance in helping me strive towards my goals.

I also thank BPB Publications for their expert guidance in bringing this book to fruition. The journey of writing this book was made possible through the invaluable participation and collaboration of the reviewers, technical experts, and editors.

I want to acknowledge and extend my gratitude to Dr. Saloni Bhushan for her valuable contributions and continuous support. Furthermore, I feel blessed to have students like Diya Gosign and Sahil Karki, who provided support whenever needed during the whole process.

Finally, I thank all the readers who have shown interest in my book and supported its realization. Your encouragement has truly been invaluable in making this endeavor a reality.

Preface

Unlock the power of PHP with this comprehensive guide to advanced web development techniques and secure coding practices. As one of the most popular programming languages for web development, PHP offers immense potential for building dynamic and feature-rich websites. This book is designed to help intermediate to advanced PHP developers harness that power and take their skills to new heights, providing insights into advanced concepts and practical strategies for creating robust, secure, and high-performing web applications.

In this book, you will embark on a journey through key chapters that cover a wide range of topics. Starting with an exploration of PHP 8's latest features and enhancements, you will learn how to leverage them to improve performance and productivity. Dive into object-oriented programming and discover how to design scalable and maintainable code structures. Delve into database integration and learn techniques for managing and optimizing database interactions. Secure coding practices are emphasized throughout, covering topics such as input validation, session management, and protection against common web vulnerabilities. Each chapter is filled with practical examples, code snippets, and exercises to reinforce your learning.

By the end of this book, you will emerge as a competent PHP developer equipped with advanced web development skills and a deep understanding of secure coding practices. You will have the knowledge and confidence to build sophisticated web applications, utilizing PHP's advanced features and industry best practices. Whether you are looking to enhance your career prospects, expand your freelance opportunities, or simply strengthen your expertise in PHP, this book is your essential companion.

Reveal the full potential of PHP and empower yourself to create secure, scalable, and high-performing websites that meet the demands of modern web development. I hope you will find this book informative and helpful.

Section - I: Fundamentals of PHP Development

Chapter 1: Introduction to Web Application- The chapter presents a comprehensive understanding of client-side scripting, server-side scripting, web servers, and the installation process of XAMPP. By the end of this chapter, readers should be able to define and differentiate between client-side scripting and server-side scripting. The reader should be able to use cases where server-side scripting is beneficial and should be able to gain knowledge about web server and their significance in hosting websites.

This chapter is providing the process of set up XAMPP on their own systems for local web development purposes.

Chapter 2: Introduction to PHP - The chapter provides a comprehensive introduction to PHP by discussing its advantages, history, setting up a development environment, essential elements for executing PHP scripts, the working of PHP, its lexical structure, case sensitivity, keywords, and the basic building blocks of PHP.

Chapter 3: PHP Basics- The chapter aims to equip learners with essential PHP programming skills. It covers the concepts of variables, constants, data types, and type manipulation. Participants will learn about operators, expressions, and the significance of comments. The chapter also focuses on control structures, break, and continue statements, enabling learners to manage program flow efficiently. Additionally, it introduces functions, teaching learners how to define, call, and use default parameters and various parameter-passing methods.

Chapter 4: PHP Arrays- The chapter provides a comprehensive understanding of arrays in PHP and various array-related functions. In this chapter, we will explore how to work with arrays, including functions for creating, manipulating, and extracting data from arrays. We will explore into the array functions available in PHP, which can be used for tasks like sorting elements, adding or removing elements, shifting elements, and reversing the order of arrays.

Section - II: Web Development with PHP

Chapter 5: PHP Forms and User Input- The chapter works towards equipping the readers with the knowledge and skills to create captivating webpages enriched with Graphical User Interface (GUI) components. Through a step-by-step approach, you will journey from designing interactive forms to effectively processing user input, enhancing your ability to build dynamic and engaging web applications.

Chapter 6: PHP Strings- The chapter presents a comprehensive understanding of PHP strings and the functions associated with them. By the end of this chapter, you will have a solid grasp of how to create, manipulate, and utilize strings in PHP, as well as a deep dive into the array of built-in string functions that PHP offers.

Chapter 7: PHP File Handling- The chapter presents a comprehensive understanding of file handling in PHP, with a focus on exploring the essential file functions and techniques.

Chapter 8: PHP Database Operations- The chapter presents a comprehensive understanding of databases and their role in software development. We begin by introducing the concept of databases and their significance in storing, managing, and retrieving structured data. Subsequently, we explore various database operations, emphasizing the importance of data manipulation, retrieval, and maintenance. The chapter then explores into practical aspects, guiding readers on how to create database tables using PHP and establish connections to MySQL databases.

Section - III: Advanced PHP Concepts and Best Practices

Chapter 9: Object-Oriented Programming in PHP- The chapter presents a comprehensive understanding of Object-Oriented Programming concepts in PHP. It covers the creation and usage of classes and objects, defining properties and methods, and explores essential OOP principles such as encapsulation, access specifiers, and the 'this' variable.

Chapter 10: PHP Security- The chapter presents a comprehensive understanding of PHP security and best practices for safeguarding web applications. It begins by addressing common security threats prevalent in PHP applications raising awareness of potential vulnerabilities.

Chapter 11: PHP Best Practices and Advanced Topics- The chapter aims to equip readers with an in-depth understanding of sophisticated PHP development techniques, emphasizing code organization, use of modern PHP versions debugging, and error handling.

Code Bundle and Coloured Images

Please follow the link to download the
Code Bundle and the ***Coloured Images*** of the book:

https://rebrand.ly/olp79kj

The code bundle for the book is also hosted on GitHub at
https://github.com/bpbpublications/Building-Dynamic-Web-Experiences-with-PHP
In case there's an update to the code, it will be updated on the existing GitHub repository.

We have code bundles from our rich catalogue of books and videos available at **https://github.com/bpbpublications**. Check them out!

Errata

We take immense pride in our work at BPB Publications and follow best practices to ensure the accuracy of our content to provide with an indulging reading experience to our subscribers. Our readers are our mirrors, and we use their inputs to reflect and improve upon human errors, if any, that may have occurred during the publishing processes involved. To let us maintain the quality and help us reach out to any readers who might be having difficulties due to any unforeseen errors, please write to us at :

errata@bpbonline.com

Your support, suggestions and feedbacks are highly appreciated by the BPB Publications' Family.

Piracy

If you come across any illegal copies of our works in any form on the internet, we would be grateful if you would provide us with the location address or website name. Please contact us at **business@bpbonline.com** with a link to the material.

If you are interested in becoming an author

If there is a topic that you have expertise in, and you are interested in either writing or contributing to a book, please visit **www.bpbonline.com**. We have worked with thousands of developers and tech professionals, just like you, to help them share their insights with the global tech community. You can make a general application, apply for a specific hot topic that we are recruiting an author for, or submit your own idea.

Reviews

Please leave a review. Once you have read and used this book, why not leave a review on the site that you purchased it from? Potential readers can then see and use your unbiased opinion to make purchase decisions. We at BPB can understand what you think about our products, and our authors can see your feedback on their book. Thank you!

For more information about BPB, please visit **www.bpbonline.com**.

Join our book's Discord space

Join the book's Discord Workspace for Latest updates, Offers, Tech happenings around the world, New Release and Sessions with the Authors:

https://discord.bpbonline.com

Table of Contents

Section - I

Fundamentals of PHP Development

CHAPTER 1
Introduction to Web Application

Introduction

A web application is a software program that runs on a web server and is retrieved by users through a web browser. It delivers interactive functionality, processes data, and delivers content over the Internet.

Web applications are built using a combination of front-end and back-end technologies. The front-end is responsible for the user interface, including the layout, design, and user interaction elements. This is typically implemented using HTML, CSS, and JavaScript.

The backend of a web application handles the logic and data processing. It consists of a server-side programming language (Python, Ruby, PHP, or JavaScript with Node.js) and a database system (MySQL, PostgreSQL, or MongoDB) for storing and retrieving data.

Structure

The chapter covers the following topics:

- Features of Web applications
- Categories of Web applications
  - Client-Side Scripting
  - Server-side Scripting

- Web servers
- Local server
- Remote server
- Dynamic website

- WAMP, LAMP, XAMPP, and MAMP Server
    - WAMP for Windows operating system
    - LAMP for Linux operating system
    - XAMPP for cross platform
    - MAMP for macOS
    - The installation process of XAMPP

Objectives

The objective of this chapter is to provide a comprehensive understanding of client-side scripting, server-side scripting, web servers, and the installation process of XAMPP. By the end of this chapter, readers should be able to define and differentiate between client-side scripting and server-side scripting. The reader should be able to use cases where server-side scripting is beneficial and should be able to gain knowledge about web server and their significance in hosting websites.

This chapter provides the process of setting up XAMPP on their own systems for local web development purposes.

Features of web applications

Web applications range from simple websites with static content to complex, dynamic applications with advanced functionality. They can be used for various purposes, including e-commerce, social networking, content management, online banking, and more.

The following are the features of a web application:

- **Accessibility:** Web applications can be accessed from anywhere with an internet connection, making them available to a wide range of users.
- **Cross-platform compatibility:** Web applications can be accessed on different devices and operating systems, including desktop computers, laptops, smartphones, and tablets.
- **Interactivity:** Users can interact with web applications by submitting forms, clicking buttons, and performing various actions, resulting in dynamic and personalized experiences.

- **Scalability:** Web applications can handle many simultaneous users and accommodate increased traffic by scaling up server resources.
- **Updates and maintenance:** Web applications can be easily updated and maintained by making changes on the server side, ensuring that all users have access to the latest version without needing to install updates.

Thus, web applications are powerful software applications accessed through web browsers, providing interactive functionality and delivering content and services to users over the Internet.

Categories of Web applications

Web applications can be categorized based on various criteria. Here are some common categories of web applications:

- **E-commerce applications**: These web applications facilitate the online buying and selling of products or services. They typically include features like product catalogs, shopping carts, payment gateways, and order processing.
- **Social media applications**: Social media applications allow users to connect, share content, and interact with others online. For example, Facebook, Twitter, Instagram, and LinkedIn.
- **Content management systems (CMS)**: CMS applications enable the creation, management, and publication of digital content. They are used for building websites, blogs, and online portals. Popular CMS platforms include WordPress, Drupal, and Joomla.
- **Online banking and financial applications**: These applications provide secure access to banking services, allowing users to perform transactions, check balances, and manage their finances online.
- **Online learning and E-Learning platforms**: E-learning applications facilitate remote learning by providing educational materials, courses, quizzes, and interactive content. Examples include platforms like Coursera, Udemy, and Khan Academy.
- **Booking and reservation systems**: These applications allow users to book and manage appointments, reservations, and tickets online. They are commonly used in industries such as travel, hospitality, and healthcare.
- **Collaboration and Project Management Tools**: These web applications help teams collaborate, manage tasks, and track projects. Examples include Trello, Asana, and Basecamp.
- **Customer Relationship Management (CRM) Systems**: CRM applications help businesses manage their interactions and relationships with customers. They typically include features for sales tracking, lead management, and customer support.

- **Gaming and Entertainment Applications**: Web-based games and entertainment applications offer interactive experiences, such as multiplayer games, online casinos, and streaming platforms like Netflix or YouTube.
- **Utility applications**: These applications provide specific services or utilities, such as weather forecasts, language translation, file conversion, or image editing.

These categories are not exhaustive, and many web applications may fall into multiple categories or have unique characteristics. The classification of web applications can vary based on the context and the specific functionality they provide.

Client-side scripting

Client-side scripting refers to the execution of scripts or code on the client's computer or device, typically within a web browser. It allows websites and web applications to enhance interactivity and perform dynamic tasks directly on the client side without relying on constant communication with the server.

The following are some key aspects of client-side scripting:

- **Programming languages:** Client-side scripting languages primarily include JavaScript, HTML, and CSS. JavaScript is the most widely used language for client-side scripting as it provides extensive capabilities for manipulating web page elements, handling user interactions, and making asynchronous requests to servers.
- **Browser execution:** The client-side scripts are executed by the web browser on the client's machine. When a user visits a website, the browser downloads the HTML, CSS, and JavaScript files associated with the page. The browser then interprets and executes the JavaScript code to render dynamic content and perform various actions.
- **Enhanced user experience:** Client-side scripting enables dynamic content updates and interactive features, enhancing the user experience of a website or web application. It allows developers to create responsive interfaces, validate user inputs, implement animations, and provide real-time feedback to users without requiring page reloads.
- **DOM manipulation:** The **Document Object Model** (**DOM**) represents the structure of an HTML document as a tree-like structure. Client-side scripting often involves manipulating the DOM using JavaScript to dynamically add, remove, or modify elements on a web page. This enables developers to create interactive elements and update the content based on user actions or other events.
- **Form validation:** Client-side scripting is commonly used for validating user inputs on web forms before submitting them to the server. JavaScript can be employed to perform checks such as verifying required fields, validating email addresses, and ensuring data format correctness. This helps prevent unnecessary server requests and provides instant feedback to users.

- **Asynchronous operations:** With client-side scripting, JavaScript can make asynchronous requests to the server, retrieve data, and update the web page without requiring a full page reload. This is often done using techniques like **Asynchronous JavaScript and XML (AJAX)** or more modern approaches like Fetch API or Axios. Asynchronous operations enable dynamic content loading, real-time updates, and interactive features.
- **Browser compatibility:** While JavaScript is supported by almost all modern web browsers, there may be slight differences in how each browser interprets and executes the code. Developers need to consider browser compatibility issues and ensure their client-side scripts work correctly across different browsers and versions.

  It is important to note that client-side scripting has certain limitations and security considerations. For example, since the code is executed on the client's machine, it can be modified or exploited by malicious users. Therefore, it is crucial to implement proper input validation, data sanitization, and security measures to mitigate potential risks.

Server-side Scripting

Server-side scripting refers to the execution of scripts on a web server in response to client requests. It involves writing code that runs on the server to generate dynamic web pages or perform various tasks, such as processing form data, interacting with databases, and generating dynamic content.

When a user sends a request to a website, the server processes the request and generates a response. In the case of server-side scripting, the server executes scripts written in languages like PHP, Python, Ruby, or ASP.NET to generate the response. The server processes the script, performs any necessary computations or database operations, and generates the resulting HTML, CSS, or other types of content, which is then sent back to the client's web browser.

Server-side scripting allows websites to be more interactive and dynamic by enabling tasks to be performed on the server before sending the response to the client. It is commonly used for building web applications, handling user authentication, managing sessions, and accessing databases. This approach provides a way to separate the presentation logic (HTML, CSS) from the business logic (scripting code) and enables more powerful and complex functionality to be implemented on the server side.

Web servers

A web server is a computer program or a hardware device that delivers web pages, files, and other content to clients over the Internet. It acts as the central processing unit for handling requests from clients (such as web browsers) and sending back the requested data.

The primary function of a web server is to store and serve web pages and other resources upon receiving requests from clients. When a user enters a website URL or clicks on a link, their web browser sends a request to the appropriate web server. The server then processes the request, retrieves the requested files or data, and sends them back to the client, which renders and displays the content in the user's browser.

Web servers typically use the **Hypertext Transfer Protocol** (**HTTP**) to communicate with clients and deliver web content. They can support various programming languages and technologies for generating dynamic web pages, such as PHP, Python, Java, or ASP.NET. Additionally, web servers may also handle other protocols, such as HTTPS for secure connections, FTP for file transfers, or SMTP for email handling.

Some popular web server software includes Apache HTTP Server, Nginx, Microsoft, **Internet Information Services** (**IIS**), and **Google Web Server** (**GWS**). These servers can be hosted on dedicated hardware or run on virtual servers or cloud platforms, providing scalability and reliable access to web content.

Local server

A local server refers to a server that is set up and operated on a local network or a single computer system. It serves web pages and other content within the local environment without being accessible from the Internet.

Unlike a publicly accessible web server, a local server is limited to serving content and handling requests within the network it is connected to. It is commonly used for development, testing, and hosting websites or web applications in a controlled environment before deploying them to a live server.

Local servers can be set up using software packages specifically designed for this purpose, such as XAMPP, WAMP, or MAMP. These packages include a combination of web server software (such as Apache or Nginx), a database management system (like MySQL or PostgreSQL), and other necessary components for running web applications locally.

By installing and configuring a local server on a computer, developers can simulate a production environment on their own machines. This allows them to test and debug their web applications, make modifications, and experiment with different configurations without affecting the live website or risking any potential security concerns associated with publicly accessible servers.

Local servers are commonly used by web developers, designers, and software engineers during the development phase to ensure the functionality and performance of their applications before deploying them to a remote or public server for wider access.

Remote server

A remote server, also known as a remote host or a remote machine, refers to a server or computer system that is located at a different physical location or network than the user's local machine. It is accessed and managed over a network, typically the Internet, through various remote access protocols. It provides various services, resources, or data to users or clients over a network.

Remote servers provide services, resources, and computing power to users who may not have physical access to them. These servers are commonly used for hosting websites, storing data, running applications, and performing various computational tasks. They can be owned and maintained by individuals, organizations, or service providers.

To interact with a remote server, users typically utilize remote access protocols such as **Secure Shell (SSH)**, **Remote Desktop Protocol** (**RDP**), or **Virtual Network Computing** (**VNC**). These protocols allow users to establish a remote connection with the server, granting them access to the server's resources and capabilities as if they were physically present.

Remote servers offer several advantages, including:

- **Accessibility**: Users can access and manage their server resources from anywhere with an internet connection, enabling remote work and administration.
- **Scalability**: Remote servers can be easily scaled up or down to accommodate changing resource requirements, allowing users to allocate computing power and storage as needed.
- **Reliability**: Remote servers are often housed in data centers with robust infrastructure, backup power, and network connectivity, providing a high level of reliability and uptime.
- **Security**: By using secure remote access protocols and implementing appropriate security measures, remote servers can offer enhanced data security and protection against physical threats.

Remote servers are commonly used by businesses, developers, and individuals who require access to powerful computing resources, centralized data storage, or the ability to host websites and online applications. They provide a flexible and efficient solution for various computing needs without the need for physical proximity to the server.

Unlike a local server that operates within a specific local network, a remote server can be accessed from anywhere with a network connection. Remote servers are often housed in data centers or cloud computing infrastructure managed by hosting providers.

Remote servers offer a wide range of services and functions, depending on their configuration and purpose. Some common types of remote servers include:

- **Web servers**: These servers host websites, web applications, and associated files and deliver them to users' web browsers upon request.
- **File servers**: They provide remote storage and file-sharing capabilities, allowing users to access and share files over a network.

- **Database servers:** These servers store and manage databases, allowing remote clients to query and manipulate data.
- **Email servers:** They handle email communication, storing, sending, and receiving email messages.
- **Application servers:** These servers host and execute applications or software programs remotely, providing services or functionality to clients over a network.

Remote servers are particularly useful for businesses, organizations, and individuals who require reliable access to resources, data, or services from different locations. They enable remote collaboration, data storage, application hosting, and other networking capabilities without the need for physical proximity to the server itself.

Static website

A static website is a type of website that consists of web pages with fixed content that remains the same for all visitors. The content of a static website is created and stored in HTML files, which are served to users exactly as they are without any modification or customization based on user interactions or data changes.

The main characteristics of a static website include:

- **Fixed content**: The content of each web page is predetermined and does not change based on user input or other external factors.
- **Limited interactivity**: Static websites generally offer limited interactive elements, such as navigation menus or clickable links, but they do not provide complex functionalities like user registration, commenting systems, or real-time updates.
- **Fast loading times**: Since the content is pre-rendered and stored as HTML files, static websites typically load quickly as there is no need for server-side processing or database queries.
- **Easy to create and host**: Static websites are relatively simple to create and can be hosted on basic web servers or even on free hosting services.
- **Lower maintenance requirements**: Once the static website is built, updates usually require manual editing of the HTML files and uploading them to the server.

Static websites are commonly used for showcasing information that does not frequently change, such as company brochures, portfolios, product catalogs, or event announcements. They are suitable for situations where interactivity or real-time data updates are not necessary and where simplicity, speed, and low hosting costs are preferred.

Dynamic website

A dynamic website is a type of website that generates and displays content that can change in real-time based on user interactions, data inputs, or other dynamic factors. Unlike static websites that serve fixed content, dynamic websites use server-side scripting languages, databases, and other technologies to dynamically generate web pages and respond to user requests.

Key features and characteristics of dynamic websites include:

- **Customized content**: Dynamic websites can generate personalized content for each user based on their preferences, settings, or input. This allows for a more interactive and tailored user experience.
- **Database integration**: Dynamic websites often utilize databases to store and retrieve data. User input can be stored in a database, and the website can fetch and display relevant information dynamically.
- **User interactivity**: Dynamic websites enable user interactions such as form submissions, user registrations, commenting systems, search functionalities, and more. These interactions trigger server-side processing and dynamic content generation.
- **Real-time updates**: Dynamic websites can display real-time information from external sources, such as stock market data, weather updates, or social media feeds. The content is updated dynamically without requiring manual intervention.
- **CMS:** Dynamic websites are frequently built using CMS platforms that provide an interface for content authors and administrators to manage and update the website content without extensive coding knowledge.

Dynamic websites are commonly used for e-commerce sites, social media platforms, news portals, online forums, web applications, and other interactive online services. They offer greater flexibility, interactivity, and the ability to handle complex functionalities compared to static websites. However, dynamic websites generally require more server resources, scripting knowledge, and ongoing maintenance compared to their static counterparts.

The main difference between a static website and a dynamic website lies in the content and interactivity they offer.

Static website vs. dynamic website

The following section differentiates between static and dynamic websites:

Based on content:

- **Static website:** A static website contains fixed content that remains the same for all visitors. The content is pre-designed and stored in HTML files, which are served to users without any modifications. Updates to a static website typically involve manual editing and republishing of the HTML files.
- **Dynamic website:** A dynamic website generates content on the fly, often retrieving information from databases or external sources. The content can change based

on user interactions, data inputs, or real-time updates. Updates to a dynamic website can be made through a content management system or by modifying the underlying scripting code.

Based on Interactivity:

- **Static website:** Static websites have limited interactivity. They can include basic interactive elements such as navigation menus or clickable links, but they generally lack complex functionalities like user registration, comment sections, or real-time updates.
- **Dynamic website:** Dynamic websites offer a higher level of interactivity. They can provide features like user registration and authentication, interactive forms, commenting systems, personalized content based on user preferences, real-time data updates, and more.

Based on data handling:

- **Static website:** Static websites do not typically handle user input or store user-specific data. They primarily serve as an informational platform where users consume pre-existing content.
- **Dynamic website:** Dynamic websites can handle user input, process form submissions, store user data in databases, and retrieve and display relevant information dynamically. They can provide personalized experiences and user-specific content and interact with external APIs or databases.

So, a static website is suitable for displaying fixed content without much interactivity, while a dynamic website is more interactive, generates content dynamically, and can handle user input and data processing. The choice between a static or dynamic website depends on the specific requirements, desired functionalities, and the level of interactivity and personalization needed for the website.

WAMP, LAMP, XAMPP, and MAMP server

WAMP, LAMP, XAMPP, and MAMP are popular server software stacks used for web development and hosting. They provide a complete environment for running web applications on a local machine. These server software stacks come bundled with all the necessary components for web development, including web servers, database servers, and scripting languages. They make it easier for developers to set up a local development environment for testing and building web applications. Each stack provides a pre-configured package, simplifying the installation and configuration process. Developers can choose the stack that aligns with their operating system and development needs.

WAMP, LAMP, XAMPP, and MAMP are software stacks that provide a bundled package of web server software, database management system, and scripting language support. They are commonly used for developing and running web applications on local machines for testing and development purposes. Let us take a closer look at each of these server stacks.

WAMP for Windows operating systems

WAMP stands for Windows, Apache, MySQL, and PHP/Perl/Python. It is a software stack specifically designed for Windows operating systems.

- **Apache**: It is the web server software responsible for serving web pages and handling HTTP requests.
- **MySQL:** It is the database management system used for storing and managing data.
- **PHP/Perl/Python:** These scripting languages are supported by WAMP to create dynamic web pages and interact with the database.

LAMP for Linux operating systems

LAMP stands for Linux, Apache, MySQL, and PHP/Perl/Python. It is similar to WAMP but is intended for Linux operating systems.

- **Linux:** It is the operating system that forms the foundation of the LAMP stack.
- **Apache:** It serves as the web server software, responsible for handling HTTP requests and delivering web pages.
- **MySQL:** It is the database management system used to store and manage data.
- **PHP/Perl/Python:** These scripting languages are supported by LAMP to create dynamic web pages and interact with the database.

XAMPP for cross-platform

XAMPP is a cross-platform software stack that stands for cross-platform (X), Apache, MySQL, PHP, and Perl.

- It is designed to work on multiple operating systems like Windows, Linux, and macOS.
- XAMPP includes Apache as the web server, MySQL as the database management system, and PHP and Perl as the supported scripting languages.
- Additionally, XAMPP also provides other components like FileZilla FTP server and phpMyAdmin for managing databases.
- XAMPP stands for Cross-Platform, Apache, MySQL, PHP, and Perl.
- It is a software stack that can be installed on multiple platforms like Windows, Linux, and macOS.

- In addition to Apache, MySQL, and PHP, XAMPP also includes Perl, which is another scripting language commonly used in web development.
- XAMPP provides an easy-to-use control panel for managing the server and its components.

MAMP for macOS

MAMP stands for macOS, Apache, MySQL, and PHP/Perl/Python.

- It is a server stack specifically designed for macOS operating systems.
- MAMP includes Apache as the web server, MySQL as the database management system, and PHP/Perl/Python as the scripting languages.
- MAMP stands for macOS, Apache, MySQL, and PHP.
- It is specifically designed for macOS operating systems.
- MAMP includes Apache as the web server, MySQL as the database management system, and PHP for server-side scripting.
- MAMP also provides an intuitive control panel for managing the server and its configurations.

These server stacks provide a convenient way to set up a local development environment for web applications. They bundle all the necessary components together, simplifying the installation and configuration process. Developers can use these stacks to develop, test, and debug their web applications locally before deploying them to a production server.

The Installation process of XAMPP

To install XAMPP, follow these steps:

1. **Download XAMPP:** Go to the official XAMPP website and download the XAMPP installer suitable for your operating system (Windows, Linux, or macOS).
2. **Run the installer:** Locate the downloaded XAMPP installer and run it. You may be prompted with security warnings or user account control prompts, so proceed accordingly.
3. **Choose components:** During the installation process, you will be asked to select which components of XAMPP you want to install. The default selection includes Apache, MySQL, PHP, and phpMyAdmin. You can choose additional components if needed. Click **Next** to continue.
4. **Choose installation folder:** Select the folder where you want to install XAMPP. The default folder is usually fine, but you can choose a different location if desired. Click **Next** to proceed.

5. **Start the installation:** Review the installation settings and click **Next** to start the installation process. Wait for the installation to complete. This may take a few minutes.

6. **Configure components:** After the installation is finished, you will be presented with configuration options. You can configure the default ports for Apache and MySQL or leave them as they are. You can also set the default language for phpMyAdmin. Make any desired changes and click **Next** to continue.

7. **Complete the installation:** Once the configuration is done, click **Finish** to complete the installation process.

8. **Start XAMPP:** After installation, you can start XAMPP by locating the XAMPP control panel application (usually found in the installation directory) and running it. The control panel allows you to start or stop the Apache and MySQL servers, as well as manage other components.

9. **Test XAMPP:** Open your web browser and enter "localhost" or "127.0.0.1" in the address bar. You should see the XAMPP welcome page indicating that the installation was successful.

XAMPP is now installed and ready for use. You can place your web files in the "htdocs" directory within the XAMPP installation folder to access them through the local server. Start Apache and MySQL through the control panel, and you can begin developing and testing your web applications locally using XAMPP.

Conclusion

In this chapter, we covered key topics related to web development, including client-side scripting, server-side scripting, web servers, local servers, remote servers, static websites, dynamic websites, and an introduction to popular server software stacks like WAMP, LAMP, XAMPP, and MAMP. We also provided a step-by-step guide to installing XAMPP.

By understanding client-side scripting, server-side scripting, and the difference between static and dynamic websites, readers gained insights into the various aspects of web development. Additionally, they learned about the role of web servers, both locally and remotely, and explored different server software options.

The chapter's installation guide for XAMPP allowed readers to set up a local server environment for web development. With this knowledge, readers are now equipped to build and deploy their own web applications using client-side and server-side scripting, utilizing the appropriate server software based on their needs and preferences.

In the next chapter, the reader will be introduced to PHP, their needs, and the history of the language.

Points to remember

- Web applications have become an essential part of modern life, enabling interactive and dynamic experiences on the **Internet**.
- Client-side scripting involves writing code on the user's web browser, often using HTML, CSS, and JavaScript.
- Server-side scripting involves writing code that executes on the web server, generating dynamic content for the client.
- Web servers are software applications that handle client requests and serve web pages to browsers.
- A local server is an environment set up on a developer's computer for testing and development purposes.
- A remote server is located in a data center or cloud environment where web applications can be hosted and accessed by users.
- Static websites are composed of fixed content that does not change unless manually updated, while dynamic websites generate content on the fly based on user interactions and data inputs.
- WAMP, LAMP, XAMPP, and MAMP are server stacks that combine Apache (**webserver**), MySQL (database management system), and PHP/Python/Perl (server-side scripting languages) to provide a development and deployment environment for web applications.
- XAMPP is a popular server stack that can be easily installed on various operating systems, including Windows, macOS, and Linux.
- When installing XAMPP, ensure that you meet the system requirements and carefully follow the installation steps provided by the XAMPP documentation.
- Remember to configure XAMPP correctly, considering security measures, server settings, and database configurations.

CHAPTER 2
Introduction to PHP

Introduction

Hypertext Pre-processor (PHP) is a popular server-side scripting language for web development. It was created in 1994 by *Rasmus Lerdorf* and has since evolved into a powerful and versatile programming language. PHP is designed specifically for web development and can be embedded within HTML code, making creating dynamic and interactive web pages easy.

Structure

In this chapter, we will cover the following topics:

- History of PHP
- Advantages of PHP
- Setting up a PHP development environment
- Elements required to execute PHP script
- Working of PHP
- Lexical structure of PHP
- PHP Case sensitivity

- Keywords of PHP
- Basic building blocks of PHP

Objectives

The objective of this chapter is to provide a comprehensive introduction to PHP by discussing its advantages, history, setting up a development environment, essential elements for executing PHP scripts, the working of PHP, its lexical structure, case sensitivity, keywords, and the basic building blocks of PHP.

History of PHP

PHP has a rich history from the mid-1990s. The following are the key milestones in the development of PHP:

- **Creation by *Rasmus Lerdorf* (1994):** PHP was created by *Rasmus Lerdorf* in 1994 as a collection of Perl scripts called *Personal Home Page Tools* to manage his website. These tools included basic functionalities for form processing and interacting with databases.

- **PHP/FI (1995-1997):** In 1995, *Lerdorf* released the next PHP version, **Personal Home Page/Forms Interpreter** (**PHP/FI**). It introduced a parser and more features, such as support for accessing databases. PHP / FI gained popularity among developers for its simplicity and effectiveness in building dynamic web pages.

- **PHP 3 (1998):** The next significant release came in June 1998 with PHP 3. This version introduced the PHP scripting language as we know it today, separating the parser and the original PHP / FI functionality. It included better support for databases, improved performance, and support for various web servers.

- **The PHP Group (2000):** In 2000, PHP development transitioned to a collaborative community effort known as *The PHP Group*. This marked the beginning of the open-source era for PHP, allowing a broader community to contribute to its development and improvement.

- **PHP 4 (2000):** PHP 4, released in May 2000, brought significant improvements, including support for **Object-Oriented Programming** (**OOP**), better performance, and increased stability. It became a widely adopted version and was the backbone of many websites and applications for several years.

- **PHP 5 (2004):** PHP 5, released in July 2004, was a major milestone in PHP's evolution. It introduced substantial improvements, including a complete rewrite of the internal engine (Zend Engine 2), native support for OOP with the introduction of classes and interfaces, improved error handling, and the addition of new features like SimpleXML and SOAP.

- **PHP 7 (2015):** PHP 7, released in December 2015, brought significant performance improvements, increased efficiency, and reduced memory consumption. It introduced the Zend Engine 3, significantly enhancing PHP's performance, making it roughly twice as fast as PHP 5. PHP 7 also introduced new features like scalar and return type declarations.
- **PHP 8 (2020):** PHP 8, released in November 2020, introduced numerous new features and improvements. It further enhanced performance, added new syntax and operators, introduced union types, and brought enhancements to error handling, JIT compilation, and more.

Throughout its history, PHP has undergone continuous development, with new releases focusing on improving performance, enhancing features, and addressing security concerns. The PHP community actively contributes to its development, ensuring its evolution to meet the evolving web development needs.

Features of PHP

PHP is a versatile scripting language used extensively in web development. Its simplicity, integration with HTML, and extensive community support have contributed to its popularity and widespread use in creating dynamic and interactive websites and web applications. Following are some of the features of PHP:

- **Server-side scripting**: PHP is executed on the server-side, meaning the PHP code is processed on the web server before being sent to the user's browser. This allows PHP to perform various tasks on the server and generate dynamic content.
- **Syntax and language features**: PHP syntax is like C, Java, and Perl, making it relatively easy to learn for developers familiar with those languages. It supports many features, including variables, data types (strings, numbers, arrays, etc.), operators, control structures (if-else statements, loops), and functions.
- **Integration with HTML**: PHP can be seamlessly integrated with HTML code. You can embed PHP code within HTML using special tags (<?php and ?>) to switch between HTML and PHP mode. This allows you to mix dynamic PHP code with static HTML content, making it easy to generate dynamic web pages.
- **Database connectivity**: PHP has built-in functions and extensions for connecting various databases, such as MySQL, PostgreSQL, and SQLite. This enables developers to interact with databases, execute queries, and retrieve or modify data.
- **Web application development**: PHP is widely used for building web applications of various sizes and complexities. It provides numerous frameworks and libraries, such as Laravel, Symfony, and CodeIgniter, which offer pre-built components and tools to streamline development and promote code reusability.

- **Server-side script execution**: PHP scripts are typically executed on the server whenever a request is made by a client (For example, a web browser). The server processes the PHP code, performs any necessary calculations or operations, and generates an HTML response that is sent back to the client.
- **Open source and community**: PHP is an open-source language, which means it is freely available and has a large community of developers contributing to its development and improvement. This active community provides extensive documentation, tutorials, and support forums, making it easier for developers to learn and troubleshoot PHP-related issues.

Advantages of PHP

PHP offers several advantages that contribute to its widespread adoption and popularity in web development. Some of the key advantages of PHP:

- **Easy to learn and use**: PHP has a relatively easy and intuitive syntax, making it accessible to developers of various skill levels. Its similarity to languages like C, Java, and Perl allows developers familiar with those languages to quickly grasp PHP concepts.
- **Large and active community**: PHP has a vast and active community of developers worldwide. This community provides extensive documentation and online resources, making finding support and solutions to coding challenges easy. Additionally, the community regularly contributes to the development of PHP, ensuring its continuous improvement.
- **Wide platform support**: PHP is compatible with various operating systems (Windows, Linux, macOS) and can run on most web servers (Apache, Nginx, IIS). This flexibility allows developers to deploy PHP applications on various platforms, making it highly versatile.
- **Integration with HTML**: PHP can be seamlessly integrated with HTML, allowing developers to embed PHP code within HTML templates. This integration simplifies the process of generating dynamic content and interacting with databases. It also facilitates the creation of reusable web components and the separation of concerns between presentation and logic.
- **Extensive database support**: PHP has built-in extensions and libraries that easily connect multiple databases, including MySQL, PostgreSQL, SQLite, and more. This makes it convenient for developers to interact with databases, execute queries, and handle data efficiently.

- **Efficient performance**: PHP is known for its efficient processing speed of web requests. It optimizes web development tasks and includes various caching mechanisms to enhance performance. Additionally, PHP 7 introduced significant performance improvements over previous versions, making it even faster.
- **Strong framework ecosystem**: PHP boasts many robust frameworks, such as Laravel, Symfony, CodeIgniter, and Zend, which provide pre-built components, tools, and architectural patterns to streamline web development. These frameworks promote code organization, scalability, and maintainability, helping developers build complex applications more efficiently.
- **Scalability and flexibility**: PHP can handle small-scale websites and large-scale applications alike. Its modular nature allows developers to add or remove functionality as needed. Additionally, PHP's ability to scale horizontally by distributing the workload across multiple servers makes it suitable for handling high-traffic and demanding environments.
- **Continuous language development**: PHP is a language that continues to evolve. Regular releases introduce new features, improvements, and security enhancements. The development community actively maintains PHP, ensuring it remains relevant and current with the latest web development trends.

These advantages make PHP popular for web development, enabling developers to build dynamic, feature-rich, and scalable applications efficiently.

Setting up a PHP development environment

Setting up a PHP development environment involves several steps to ensure you have the necessary tools and configurations. Here is a general guide to help you set up a PHP development environment:

- **Install a web server**: PHP requires a web server to run your PHP scripts. Popular options include Apache, Nginx, and Microsoft IIS. Choose a web server that suits your needs and follow the installation instructions for your operating system.
- **Installing PHP on Windows:**

  Follow the below steps to install PHP on Windows:

1. Visit **https://www.php.net/** website using any web browser and click on **Downloads** as can be seen in *Figure 2.1:*

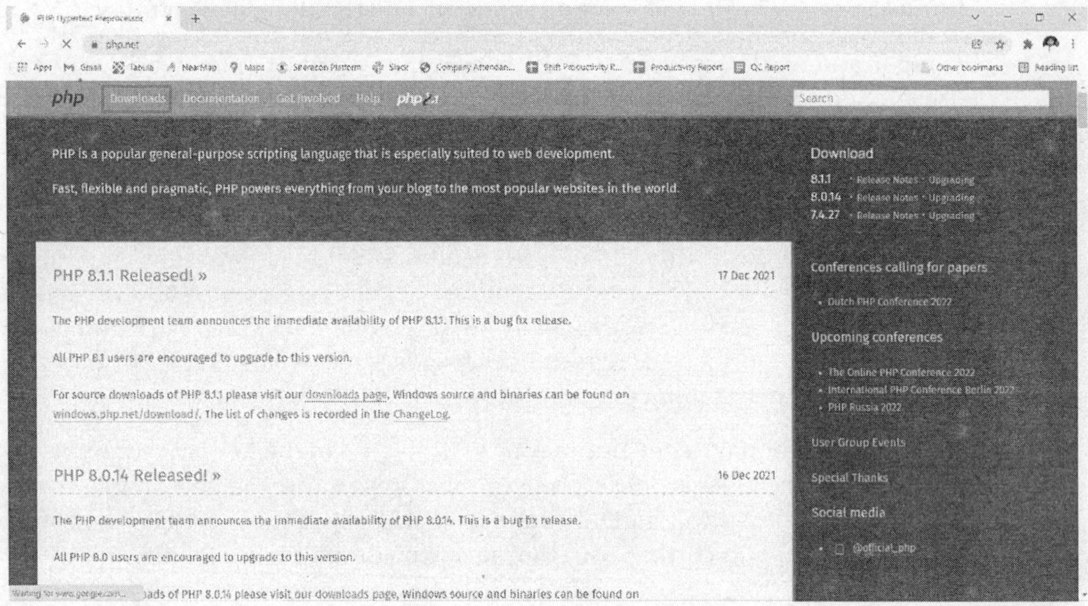

***Figure 2.1:** Download PHP*

2. Click on the Windows "**Downloads**" button as shown in *Figure 2.2:*

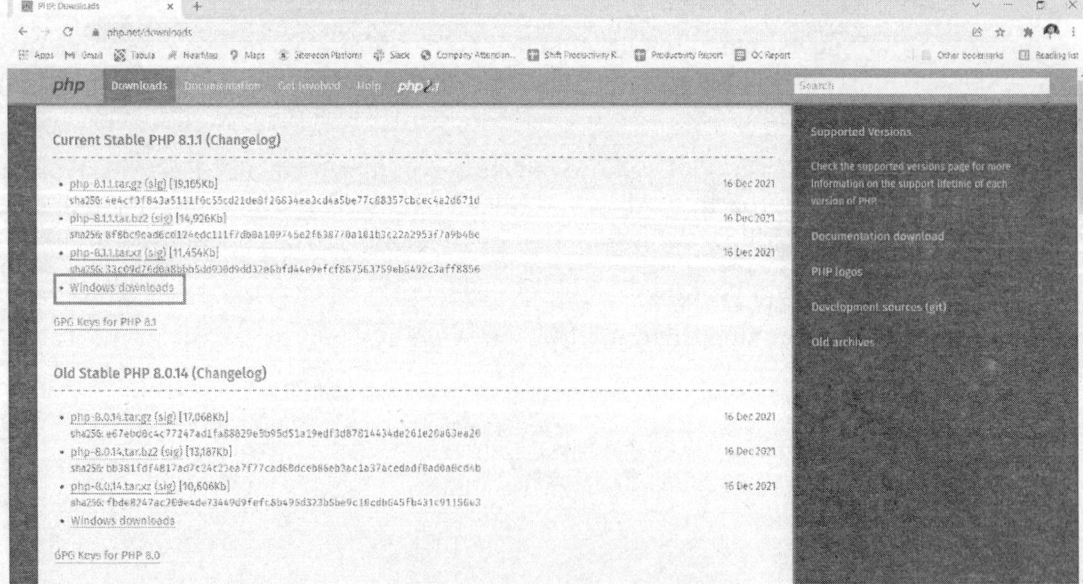

***Figure 2.2:** Windows downloads*

3. The new webpage has different options. Choose the Thread safe version, click on the zip button and download it. Refer to the following *Figure 2.3:*

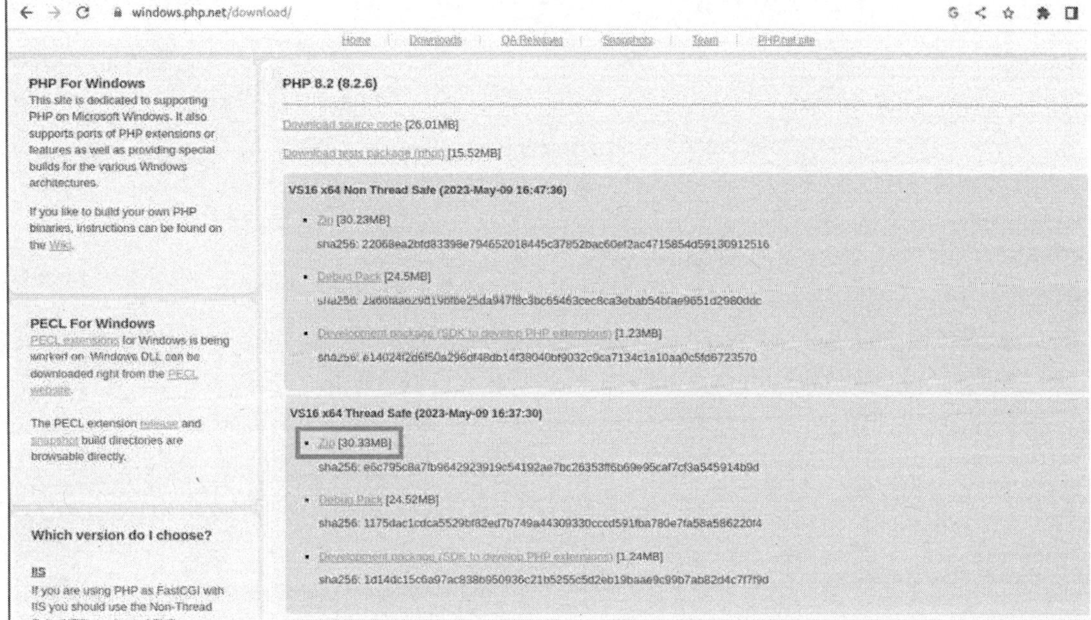

Figure 2.3: Thread safe zip folder

4. Now check for the executable file in downloads in your system and extract it (*Figure 2.4*).

Figure 2.4: Open the zip folder

5. After extracting, you get the extracted folder, as shown in the following *Figure 2.5*:

***Figure 2.5**: Extract the folder*

6. Now copy the extracted folder as seen in *Figure 2.6*:

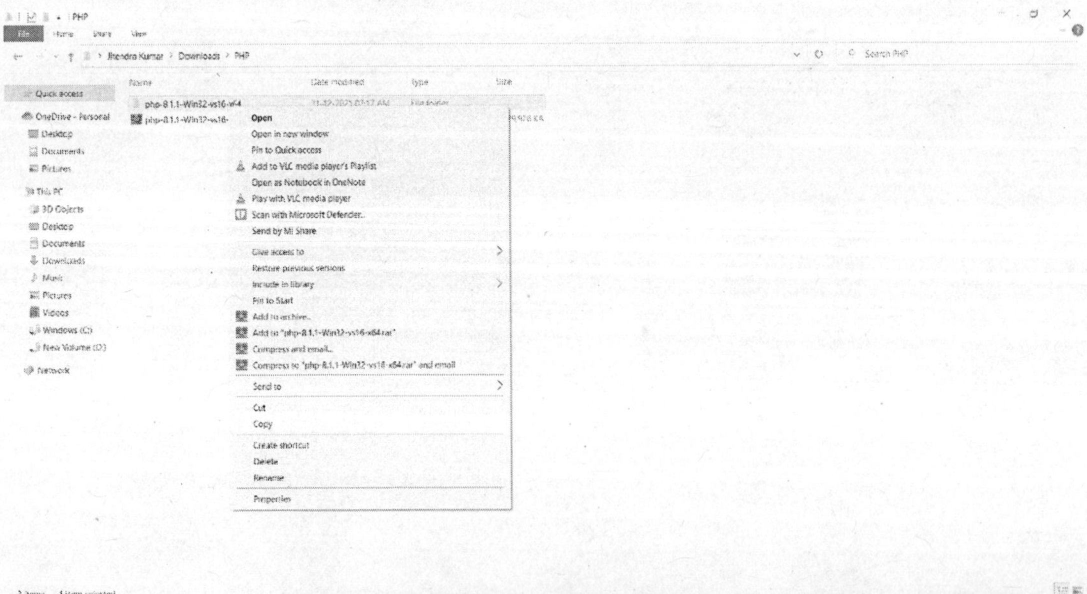

***Figure 2.6**: Copy the extracted folder by right click on it*

7. Paste the copy folder in your Windows drive in the **Program files** folder. Refer to the following *Figure 2.7:*

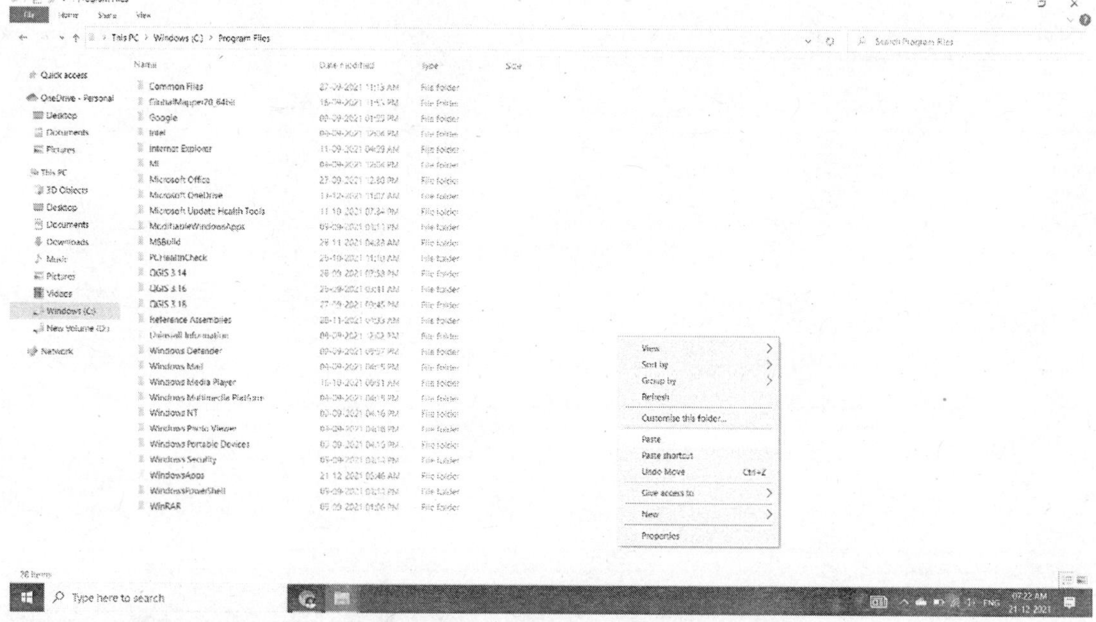

***Figure 2.7:** Paste in the program files folder*

8. Now the permission windows appears to paste the folder in program files, then click on **Continue**, as shown in *Figure 2.8:*

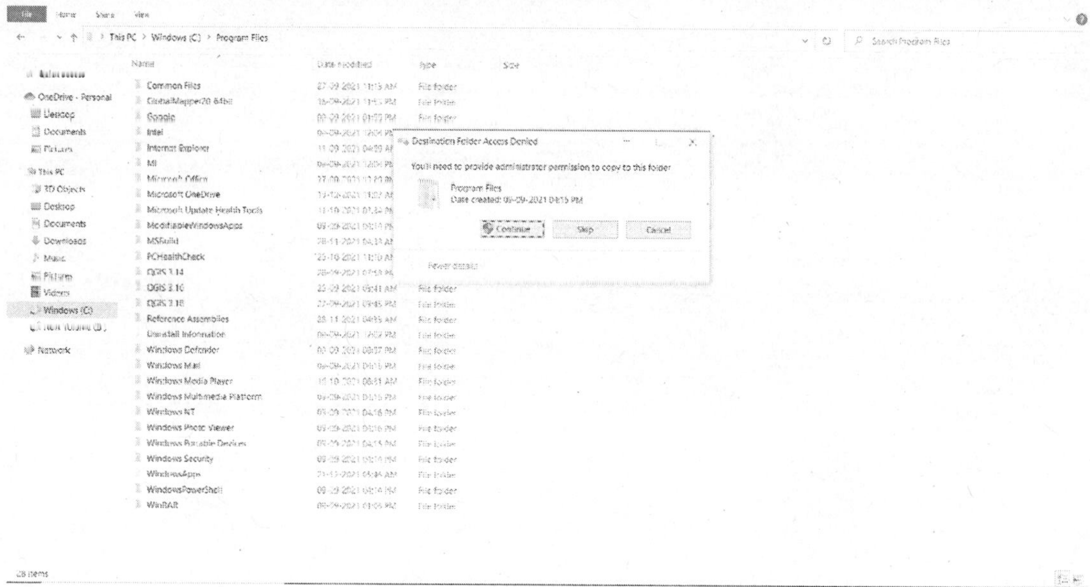

***Figure 2.8:** Click on Continue to give permission*

9. Now, after pasting the folder, copy the address of the folder in the program files, as seen in *Figure 2.9*:

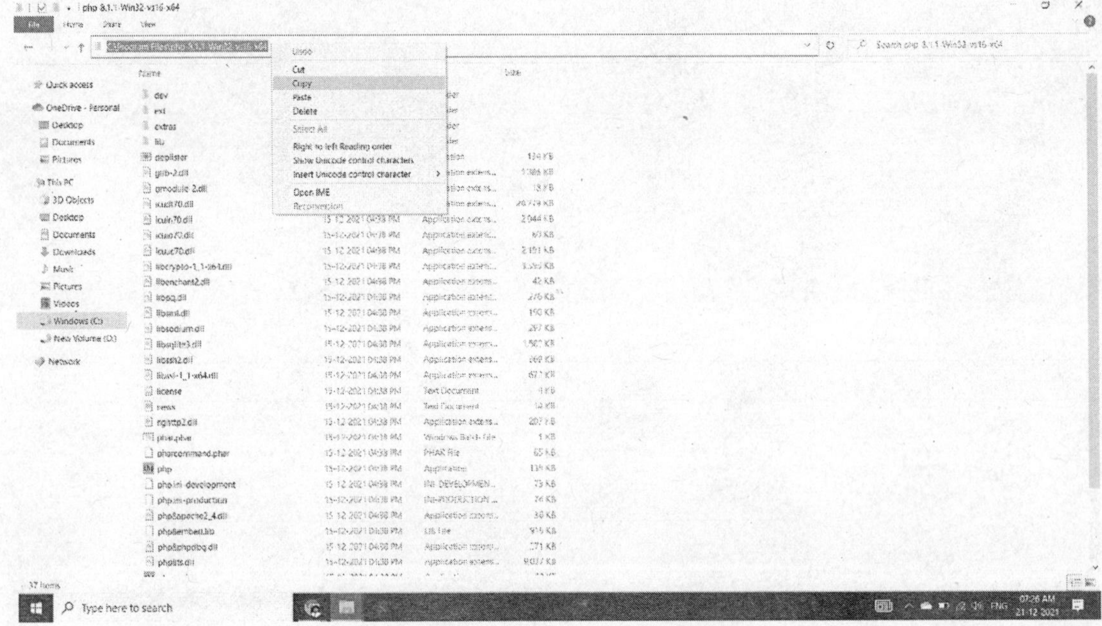

***Figure 2.9**: Copy the address of the folder*

10. Now click on Start menu and search "**Edit the system environment variables**" and open it (*Figure 2.10*).

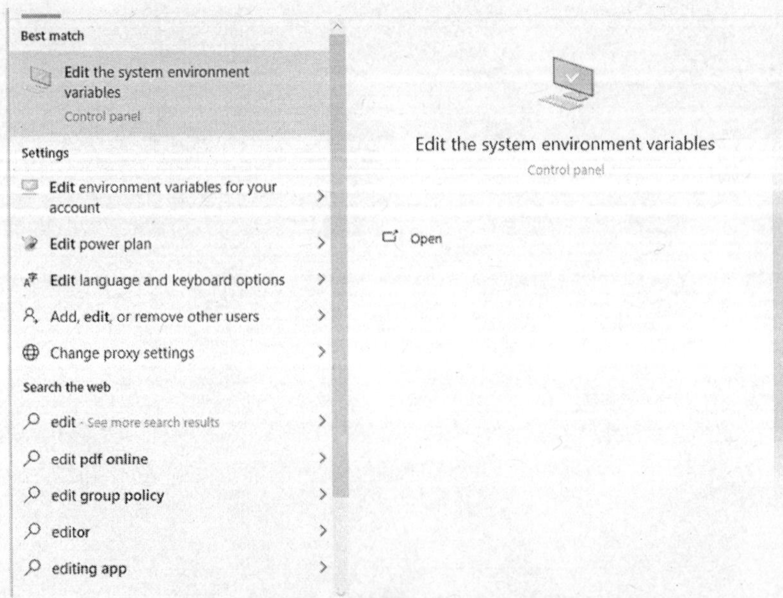

***Figure 2.10**: Search for "Edit the system environment variables"*

11. After opening System, Variable New window appears, and click on "**Environment Variables...**". Refer to the *Figure 2.11:*

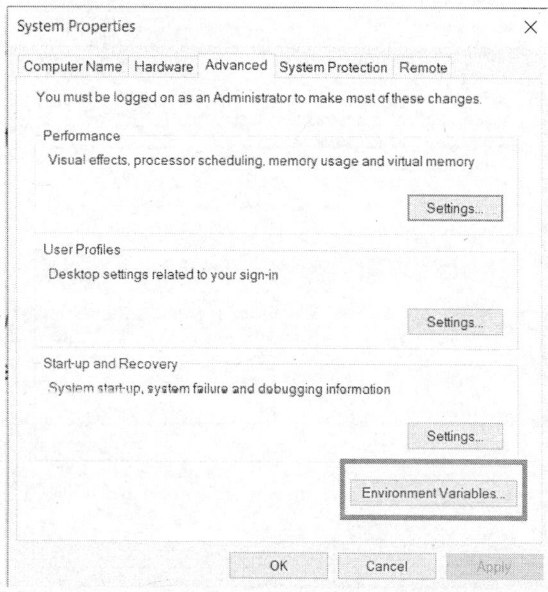

Figure 2.11*: System Properties Window*

12. Now go to the "**System variables**" *Path* option and double-click on *Path*. Refer to the following *Figure 2.12:*

Figure 2.12*: Environment Variables*

13. Next screen will open and click on the "**New**" button, as seen in *Figure 2.13*:

***Figure 2.13**: Edit environment variable*

14. After New paste the address, we copied from the program files to new and clicked on the *Enter* button (*Figure 2.14*).

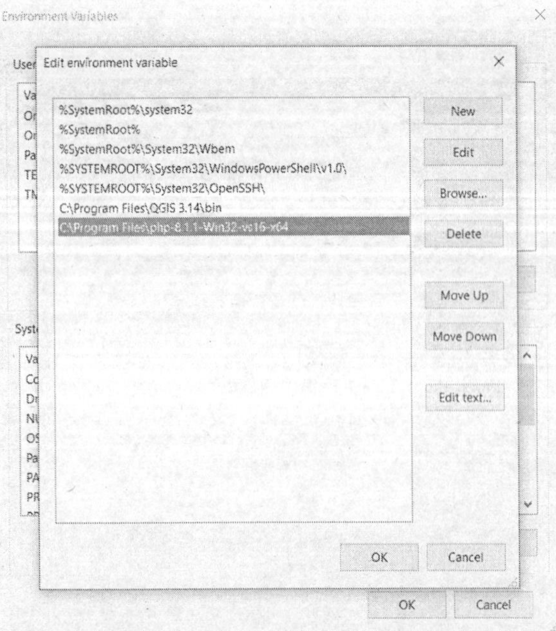

***Figure 2.14**: Edit Environment Variable*

15. Now, click on the **OK** button, as seen in *Figure 2.15*:

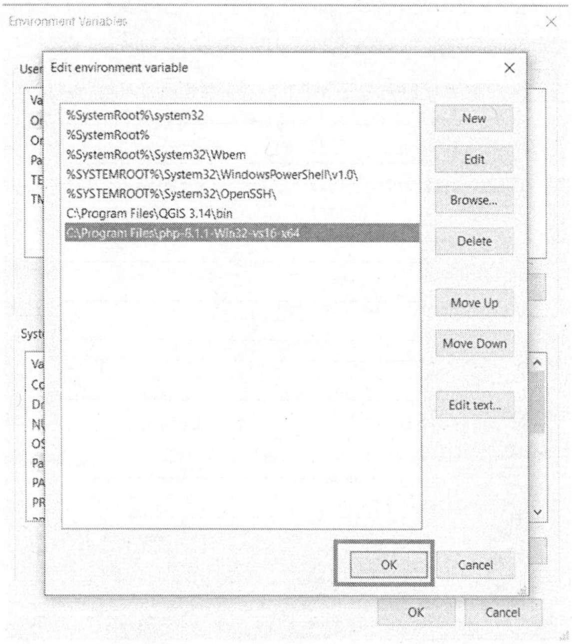

***Figure 2.15**: Edit Environment Variable*

16. Click on the **OK** button, as shown in *Figure 2.16:*

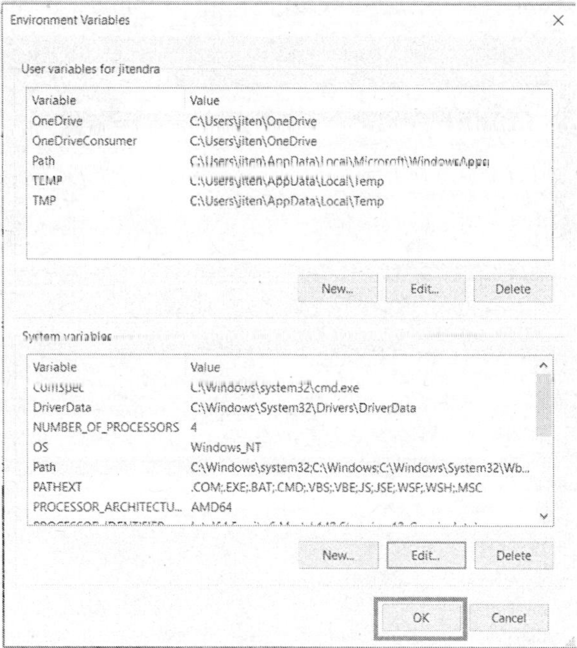

***Figure 2.16**: Environment Variable*

17. Click on **OK** for saving changes, as can be seen in *Figure 2.17:*

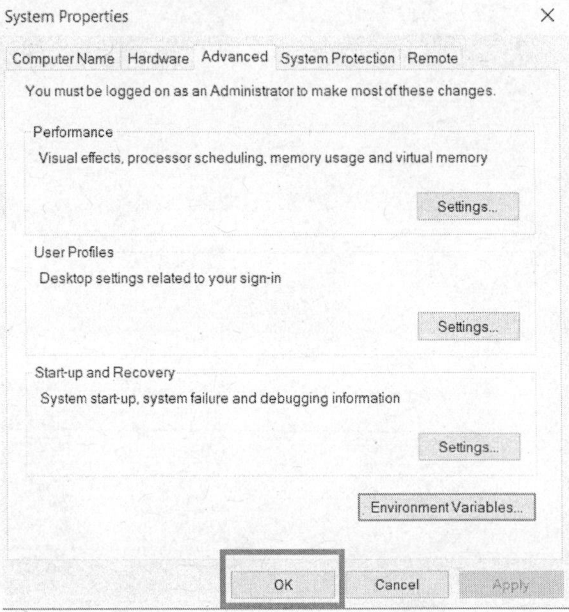

***Figure 2.17**: System properties*

18. Now, your PHP is installed on your computer. You may check by going to the "**Start**" menu and typing Command Prompt. Open it, as can be seen in *Figure 2.18*:

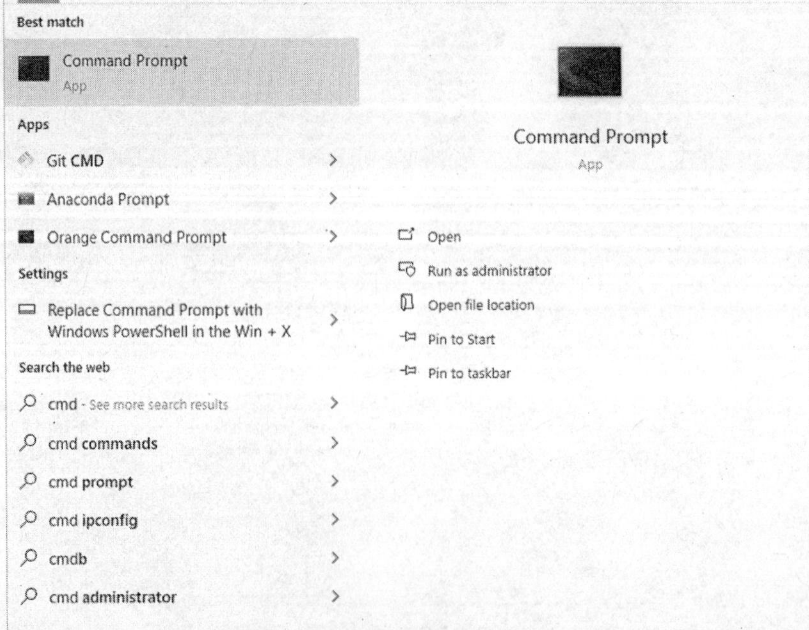

***Figure 2.18**: Command Prompt*

19. When the command prompt opens, type **php -v**, as shown in *Figure 2.19:*

```
Command Prompt
Microsoft Windows [Version 10.0.19044.1415]
(c) Microsoft Corporation. All rights reserved.

C:\Users\jiten php -v
```

***Figure 2.19**: Version Command*

20. Now enter the command prompt to show the version of PHP installed on your computer. Refer *Figure 2.20:*

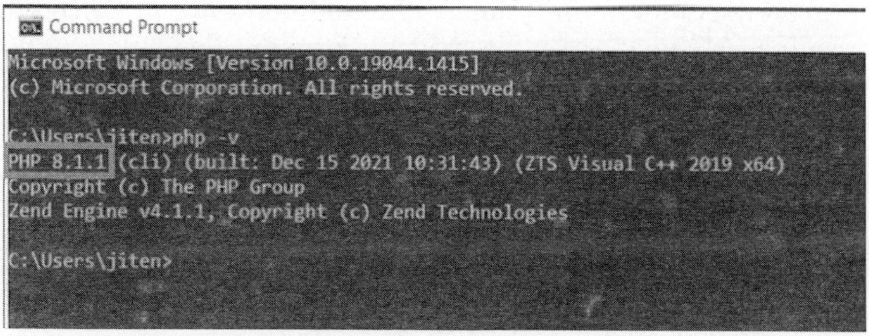

```
Command Prompt
Microsoft Windows [Version 10.0.19044.1415]
(c) Microsoft Corporation. All rights reserved.

C:\Users\jiten>php -v
PHP 8.1.1 (cli) (built: Dec 15 2021 10:31:43) (ZTS Visual C++ 2019 x64)
Copyright (c) The PHP Group
Zend Engine v4.1.1, Copyright (c) Zend Technologies

C:\Users\jiten>
```

***Figure 2.20**: Version of PHP*

You have successfully installed PHP on your Windows 10 system.

Regularly update your PHP version and related dependencies to benefit from bug fixes, security patches, and new features.

Setting up a PHP development environment may vary based on your operating system and specific requirements. It is recommended to refer to the documentation of the tools and technologies you are using for more detailed installation and configuration instructions.

Elements required to execute PHP script

PHP can work as a server-side scripting language used for application development and as a command-line programming language. But mostly, it can be used as a server-side scripting language.

To execute a PHP script, the following elements are required:

- **PHP interpreter**: You need a PHP interpreter installed on the server or your local machine to execute PHP scripts. The interpreter reads and executes the PHP code line by line.

- **PHP script**: You need a PHP script file with a `.php` extension that contains the PHP code you want to execute. You can create a PHP script using a text editor or an IDE.
- **Web server**: If you run PHP scripts on a web server, you need web server software like Apache, Nginx, or Microsoft IIS installed and properly configured. The web server listens for incoming requests, processes the PHP scripts, and sends the generated HTML or other output back to the client's browser.
- **File permissions**: Ensure that the PHP script file has appropriate permissions set so that it can be read and executed by the PHP interpreter. Generally, the file should have read and execute permissions for the PHP interpreter user.
- **Web browser or command line interface**: You can execute PHP scripts through a web browser or from the **Command Line Interface** (**CLI**). If you run the script through a web browser, you need a URL to access the PHP script file. If you use the CLI, you can run the script using the PHP command followed by the script filename.
- **Optional database connectivity**: If your PHP script interacts with a database, you may need to configure the database connection settings within your script. This involves specifying the host, username, password, and database name to establish a connection and perform database operations.

Always save the PHP script file with the `.php` extension and ensure it is in the appropriate directory accessible by the web server or CLI, depending on how you intend to execute it.

Working of PHP

PHP is a server-side scripting language for web development. It works as follows:

- **Client request**: A client, typically a web browser, sends a request to a web server for a PHP-enabled web page.
- **Web server**: The web server (for example, Apache, Nginx) receives the request and identifies that the requested file has a `.php` extension, indicating that it contains PHP code.
- **PHP interpreter**: The web server passes the PHP script to the PHP interpreter installed on the server. The PHP interpreter is responsible for executing PHP code.
- **Code execution**: The PHP interpreter reads the PHP script line by line, interprets the PHP code, and performs the requested actions. This can include a wide range of tasks, such as generating dynamic HTML content, interacting with databases, processing form data, manipulating files, and more.
- **Interacting with other technologies**: PHP can interact with various technologies and services. For example, it can connect to databases (for example, MySQL,

PostgreSQL) to retrieve or store data, communicate with external APIs, manipulate XML or JSON data, and handle user sessions and authentication.

- **Server response**: After executing the PHP code, the interpreter generates the output, which can be HTML, XML, JSON, or any other supported content type. The web server sends this output back to the client as an HTTP response.
- **Client display**: The client (web browser) receives the HTTP response containing the output generated by the PHP script. The client's browser interprets the response and displays the rendered web page to the user.

Throughout this process, PHP allows you to embed PHP code within HTML or other document types, using special delimiters like "<?php" and "?>". This makes it easy to mix dynamic server-side processing with static content.

It is important to note that PHP is not limited to web development. It can also be used for command-line scripting, server administration, and other tasks where scripting capabilities are required.

Lexical structure of PHP

The lexical structure of a programming language is the group of fundamental rules that control how one can write programs in that language. It describes things such as rules followed while naming the variable, characters that are used to specify comments in code, and how program statements are differentiated from each other, etc.

The lexical structure of PHP refers to its basic syntax and rules governing the formation of PHP code. Here are the key components of PHP's lexical structure:

- **Tags**:
  - PHP code is typically enclosed within `<?php and ?>` tags. This indicates the start and end of PHP code blocks.
  - Short tags like `<?` and `?>` can also be used if enabled in the PHP configuration, but they are not recommended for portability reasons.
- **Comments**:
  - PHP supports two types of comments:
    - **Single-line comments**: These start with // or # and continue until the end of the line.

```
// This is a single-line comment

$variable = 42; // You can add comments at the end of a line
of code
```

- **Multi-line comments**: These begin with /* and end with */, allowing comments to span multiple lines.

```
/*
This is a multi-line comment.
It can span across multiple lines.
You can comment out entire sections of code.
*/
$variable = 42;
```

- **Statements**:
  - PHP code is composed of statements, which are instructions or actions to be executed.
  - Statements are terminated with a semicolon (;), except for control structures like loops or conditional statements that use curly braces to define code blocks.
- **Variables**:
  - PHP variables are denoted by a dollar sign (**$**) followed by the variable name.
  - Variable names must start with a letter or underscore and can contain letters, numbers, or underscores. They are case-sensitive.
- **Data types**:
  - PHP supports various data types, including:
    - **Integers**: Whole numbers without a decimal point.
    - **Floating-point numbers**: Numbers with decimal points.
    - **Strings**: Sequences of characters enclosed in single or double quotes.
    - **Booleans**: Represented by the keywords **true** and **false**.
    - **Arrays**: Ordered collections of values.
    - **Objects**: Instances of classes.
    - **Null**: Represents the absence of a value.
    - **Resources**: External references to system resources.
    - **Callable**: Functions or methods that can be called.
- **Operators**:
  - PHP supports a wide range of operators, such as arithmetic, assignment, comparison, logical, and string concatenation operators.

- Arithmetic operators include +, -, *, /, % (modulus), etc.
- Assignment operators include =, +=, -=, *=, /=, etc.
- Comparison operators include ==, !=, >, <, >=, <=, etc.
- Logical operators include && (AND), | | (OR), ! (NOT), etc.

- **Control structures**:
  - PHP provides control structures to control the flow of execution, including:
    - **Conditional statements**: **if, else if, else, switch.**
    - **Looping statements**: **for, while, do-while, foreach.**
    - **Branching statements**: **break, continue, return.**
- **Functions and Classes**:
  - PHP supports defining and using functions and classes for code organization and reusability.
  - Functions are declared using the `function` keyword, followed by the function name, parameter list, and function body.
  - Classes are defined using the `class` keyword, followed by the class name, class properties, and class methods.

These are the fundamental elements that make up the lexical structure of PHP. Understanding these components is essential for writing valid and meaningful PHP code.

PHP case sensitivity

In PHP, the case sensitivity depends on the context and the elements being referenced. Here are some key points regarding case sensitivity in PHP:

- **Variables**: PHP variable names are case-sensitive. For example, `$myVariable` and `$myvariable` are considered two distinct variables.
- **Functions and language constructs**: PHP function names and language constructs (For example, `echo`, `if`, `foreach`) are not case-sensitive. You can use them in any case you prefer. For example, `echo "Hello";`, `Echo "Hello";`, and `ECHO "Hello";` are all valid.
- **Constants**: By default, PHP constants are case-sensitive. When you define a constant using the `define()` function, its name is case-sensitive by default. For example:

```
define("MY_CONSTANT", 123);
echo MY_CONSTANT;    // Outputs 123
echo My_Constant;    // Error: Undefined constant 'My_Constant'
```

However, you can use the **define()** function's third argument as **true** to make the constant case-insensitive:

```
define("MY_CONSTANT", 123, true);
echo MY_CONSTANT;    // Outputs 123
echo My_Constant;    // Outputs 123
```

- **Classes and objects**: Class names in PHP are case-insensitive when used for instantiating objects. However, the case sensitivity of class names is file-system dependent. It is recommended to follow a consistent naming convention to avoid any confusion. For example:

```
class MyClass {
   // Class implementation
}
$obj = new MyClass();   // Instantiating the object
```

  Note that the method and property names within a class are case-sensitive.

- **File names**: In most operating systems, PHP file names are case-sensitive. Therefore, when including or requiring PHP files, you need to match the exact case of the file name.

It is generally good practice to follow consistent naming conventions and be mindful of case sensitivity to avoid any potential conflicts or errors in PHP code.

Keywords of PHP

PHP has a set of reserved keywords that have predefined meanings in the language. These keywords cannot be used as identifiers (For example, variable names, function names, and class names) because they are already used by PHP for specific purposes. According to the PHP official documentation, found at_

"**https://www.php.net/manual/en/reserved.keywords.php**", the following *Table 2.1* and *Table 2.2* are some of the keywords in PHP:

`__halt_compiler()`	`abstract`	`and`	`array()`	`as`
`break`	`callable`	`case`	`catch`	`class`
`clone`	`const`	`continue`	`declared`	`default`
`die()`	`do`	`echo`	`else`	`elseif`
`empty()`	`enddeclare`	`endfor`	`endforeach`	`endif`
`endswitch`	`endwhile`	`eval()`	`exit()`	`extends`

final	finally	fn (as of PHP 7.4)	for	foreach
function	global	goto	if	implements
include	Include_once	instanceof	insteadof	interface
isset()	list()	match (as of PHP 8.0)	namespace	new
or	print	private	protected	public
readonly(as of PHP 8.1.0) *	require	Require_once	return	static
switch	throw	trait	try	unset()
use	var	while	xor	yield
yield from				

Table 2.1: Keywords of PHP

Compile-time constants					
__CLASS__	__DIR__	__FILE__	__FUNCTION__	__LINE__	__METHOD__
__NAMESPACE__	__TRAIT__				

Table 2.2: Compile-time constants

Note: readonly may be used as the function name.

Basic building blocks of PHP

The basic building blocks of PHP include the following:

- **Variables**: PHP allows you to declare variables to store and manipulate data. Variables are represented by a dollar sign ($) followed by the variable name. You can assign values to variables and retrieve their values as needed.
- **Data types**: PHP supports various data types, including integers, floating-point numbers, strings, Booleans, arrays, objects, null, resources, and callable. Each data type has specific characteristics and behaviors.
- **Operators**: PHP provides a range of operators for performing arithmetic, assignment, comparison, logical, string manipulation, and other operations. Operators allow you to combine and manipulate values and variables.
- **Control structures**: PHP offers control structures that enable you to control the flow of execution in your code. These include if statements, switch statements, loops (such as for, while, and foreach), and conditional operators (such as the ternary operator).

- **Functions**: PHP allows you to define functions, which are reusable blocks of code that perform specific tasks. Functions help in organizing code, improving code reuse, and enhancing readability. You can define your own custom functions or use built-in functions provided by PHP.
- **Arrays**: Arrays are used to store collections of values in PHP. PHP supports both indexed arrays (where values are accessed using numeric indices) and associative arrays (where values are accessed using keys). Arrays can hold values of different data types.
- **Strings**: PHP has robust string manipulation capabilities. You can use single quotes or double quotes to define strings. PHP supports various string functions for concatenation, manipulation, searching, and formatting.
- **File handling**: PHP provides functions for working with files and directories. You can read from and write to files, open and close file handles, and perform various operations related to file management.
- **Error handling**: PHP includes mechanisms for handling errors and exceptions that may occur during the execution of a PHP script. You can use error reporting functions, exception handling techniques, and custom error handlers to manage errors effectively.
- **Database connectivity**: PHP has extensive support for interacting with databases. You can connect to databases using extensions like MySQLi or PDO, execute SQL queries, fetch results, and perform database operations.

These are the fundamental building blocks of PHP that allow you to write dynamic and powerful scripts. By mastering these elements, you can create sophisticated web applications, perform data manipulation, and automate various tasks using PHP.

Conclusion

The chapter provided an overview of PHP, highlighting its advantages, history, and the process of setting up a development environment. We explored the elements required for executing PHP scripts and discussed the working of PHP, including its lexical structure, case sensitivity, and keywords. Additionally, we covered the basic building blocks of PHP, such as variables, operators, control structures, functions, classes, and file handling. By grasping these concepts, readers have gained a solid foundation for further exploration and utilization of PHP in web development.

Points to remember

- PHP is a widely used scripting language with several advantages, including its ease of use, cross-platform compatibility, and extensive community support.

- PHP was originally created by *Rasmus Lerdorf* and has evolved from a "Personal Home Page" tool into "PHP: Hypertext Pre-processor."
- To set up a PHP development environment, choose a suitable web server, install PHP, configure the server, and verify the installation by running a test script.
- The essential elements required for executing PHP scripts include a server with PHP installed, a web browser to access the script, proper file extensions, and PHP start and end tags.
- PHP scripts are embedded within HTML code and executed on the server side, with the output sent back to the client as HTML.
- Understanding the lexical structure of PHP is crucial, including knowledge of variables, data types, operators, control structures, functions, classes, comments, and whitespace.
- PHP is case-insensitive for variable names and function calls but case-sensitive for constant names and class names.
- Familiarize yourself with the keywords of PHP, which are reserved words with specific meanings in the language.
- The basic building blocks of PHP include variables and data types, operators and expressions, control structures, functions and classes, and file handling and I/O operations.

CHAPTER 3
PHP Basics

Introduction

Hypertext Preprocessor (PHP) is a widely used server-side scripting language designed for web development. Its main purpose is to generate dynamic web content and handle database interactions. PHP code is embedded within HTML, and its syntax is straightforward. Variables are declared with a dollar sign, and the language supports various data types. PHP allows control structures like if-else statements and loops for conditional logic and iteration. Custom functions can be defined to encapsulate code for reuse. PHP is often used for processing form data submitted by users and can interact with databases to store and retrieve information. It also supports object-oriented programming for organized and reusable code. Its extensive community and libraries make PHP popular for building dynamic and interactive web applications.

Structure

In this chapter, we will cover the following topics:

- Variables and constants
- Variable scope
- Data types

- Type juggling
- Type casting
- Operators and expressions
- Comments in PHP
- Control structures
- Functions
- Defining PHP function
- Calling to function
- Default parameter
- Parameter passing

Objectives

This chapter aims to equip learners with essential PHP programming skills. It covers the concepts of variables, constants, data types, and type manipulation. Participants will learn about operators, expressions, and the significance of comments. The chapter also focuses on control structures, break, and continue statements, enabling learners to manage program flow efficiently. Additionally, it introduces functions, teaching learners how to define, call, and use default parameters and various parameter-passing methods. By the end, learners will have a strong foundation to create dynamic and interactive web applications using PHP.

Variables in PHP

In PHP, variables store data and assign it a name for easy reference. Here are the key points about variables in PHP:

- **Variable declaration:** In PHP, variables are declared using the dollar sign (`$`) followed by the variable name. For example: `$name`, `$age`, `$count`.

- **Variable names:** Variable names in PHP are case-sensitive and must start with a letter or an underscore. They can contain letters, numbers, and underscores. However, using descriptive names and following naming conventions is good practice.

- **Variable assignment:** Variables are assigned values using the assignment operator (=). For example: `$name = "John";`, `$age = 25;`.

Constants in PHP

Constants in PHP are like variables, but their values cannot be changed once they are defined. They provide a way to store fixed values that remain consistent throughout the execution of a script. Defining constants in PHP is simple and can be done using the **define()** function or the **const** keyword. By convention, constant names are typically written in uppercase letters. You can access constants anywhere in your PHP code without any special syntax or scope resolution. For a comprehensive list of reserved keywords in PHP, refer to *Table 2.2* in *Chapter 2, Introduction to PHP*.

Here are the syntaxes for defining constants in PHP:

Using the define() function:

```
define('CONSTANT_NAME', value, case_insensitive);
```

CONSTANT_NAME: The name of the constant you want to define. By convention, constant names are usually uppercase.

value: The value assigned to the constant.

case_insensitive (optional): By default, constants are case-sensitive. If you set this parameter to **true**, the constant becomes case-insensitive.

Example:

```
define('MAX_LENGTH', 100);
```

Using the **const** keyword (available since PHP 5.3):

```
const CONSTANT_NAME = value;
```

CONSTANT_NAME: The name of the constant you want to define. By convention, constant names are usually uppercase.

value: The value assigned to the constant.

Example:

```
const MAX_LENGTH = 100;
```

Once a constant is defined, its value cannot be changed or redefined during the execution of the script. Constants are automatically global and can be accessed from anywhere in the PHP script without needing a global keyword.

To access the value of a constant, you can simply refer to it using its name, for example, **CONSTANT_NAME**.

Variable scope

In PHP, there are several scopes for variables:

- **Global scope**: Variables declared outside any function or class have global scope. They are accessible from anywhere within the PHP script, including inside functions and classes. You need to use the **`global`** keyword or the **`$GLOBALS`** superglobal array to access global variables within a function.

  Example:

```
$globalVariable = 10;
function myFunction() {
    global $globalVariable;
    echo $globalVariable;  // Output: 10
}
```

- **Function scope:** Variables declared within a function have function scope. They are accessible only within the function where they are declared. Function variables are created when the function is called and destroyed when the function finishes executing.

  Example:

```
function myFunction() {
    $functionVariable = 20;
    echo $functionVariable;  // Output: 20
}
myFunction();
echo $functionVariable;  // Error: Undefined variable
```

- **Static scope:** PHP allows you to declare static variables within functions. Static variables retain their values between function calls. They are accessible only within the function in which they are declared, but their values persist across multiple invocations of the function.

  Example:

```
function myFunction() {
    static $staticVariable = 30;
    echo $staticVariable;  // Output: 30
    $staticVariable++;
}
myFunction();  // Output: 30
myFunction();  // Output: 31
```

- **Class scope:** Variables declared within a class have class scope. They are accessible from within any class method using the **`$this`** keyword.

  Example:

```
class MyClass {
    public $classVariable = 40;

    public function myMethod() {
        echo $this->classVariable;  // Output: 40
    }
}
$object = new MyClass();
$object->myMethod();
```

It is important to note that PHP does not have block-level scope like some other programming languages. Variables defined within **`if`** statements, loops, or other block constructs will still be accessible outside of those blocks.

Data types in PHP

In PHP, data types define the type of data that can be stored in variables or returned by functions. PHP supports several fundamental data types, which are as discussed below, shown in *Figure 3.1*:

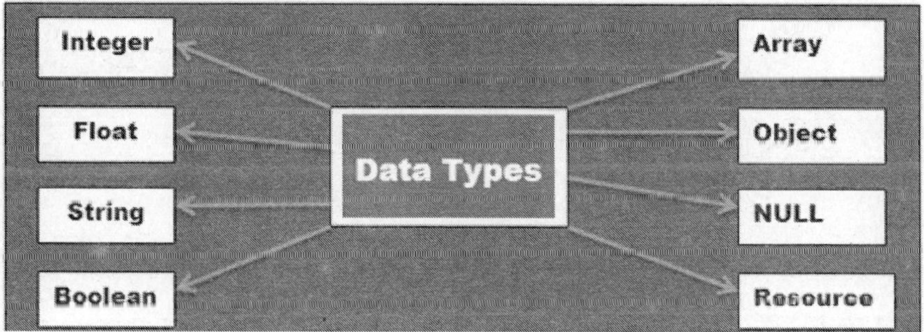

***Figure 3.1**: Data types in PHP*

- **String:** A sequence of characters enclosed in single quotes (`' '`) or double quotes (`" "`).

  Example:

```
$name = "John";
$message = 'Hello, '.$name.'!';
```

- **Integer:** Whole numbers without decimal points.

  Example:

  ```
  $age = 25;
  ```

- **Float:** Numbers with decimal points.

  Example:

  ```
  $price = 19.99;
  ```

- **Boolean:** Represents either true or false.

  Example:

  ```
  $isLogged = true;
  ```

- **Array:** Holds multiple values in an ordered collection. Arrays can store values of different data types.

  Example:

  ```
  $fruits = array("apple", "banana", "orange");
  ```

- **Object:** Instances of classes that contain properties and methods.

  Example:

  ```
  class Person {
  public $name;
  public $age;
  }
  $person = new Person();
  $person->name = "John";
  $person->age = 25;
  ```

- `NULL`: Represents a variable with no value assigned.

  Example:

  ```
  $variable = NULL;
  ```

- **Resource:** Special variables holding references to external resources, such as database connections or file handles.

  Example:

  ```
  $file = fopen("data.txt", "r");
  ```

These are the commonly used data types in PHP. Understanding their characteristics will help you manipulate and process data effectively in PHP programming.

Type juggling

Type juggling in PHP refers to the automatic conversion of variables from one data type to another by the PHP interpreter. PHP is a loosely typed language, which means it does not require explicit type declarations for variables. This allows for flexibility but can also lead to unexpected behavior if not used carefully. Following are some examples of type juggling in PHP:

- **String to Integer Conversion:** When dealing with strings containing numeric values, PHP automatically converts them to integers when needed. This enables developers to perform arithmetic operations or use numeric comparisons directly on string variables without explicit type casting.

  ```
  $number = "10"; // String
  $sum = $number + 5; // The string will be converted to an integer
  echo $sum; // Output: 15
  ```

- **Integer to String Conversion:** PHP automatically converts them to strings as required when dealing with integers. This enables developers to manipulate numeric values as strings without requiring explicit type casting.

  ```
  $age = 25; // Integer
  $message = "Your age is: " . $age; // The integer will be converted
  to a string
  echo $message; // Output: Your age is: 25
  ```

- **String to Boolean Conversion:** When dealing with strings, PHP automatically converts certain strings to Boolean values. This feature enables developers to work with string representations of true and false without explicit type casting, simplifying conditional checks and Boolean operations in PHP code.

  ```
  $text = "true"; // String
  $flag = ($text == true); // The string will be converted to a boolean
  var_dump($flag); // Output: bool(true)
  ```

- **Array to String Conversion:** When an array is treated as a string, PHP automatically concatenates its elements, providing a concise representation of the array's contents without the need for explicit type casting.

  ```
  $fruits = array("apple", "banana", "orange"); // Array
  $text = "I like " . $fruits; // The array will be converted to a
  string
  echo $text; // Output: I like Array
  ```

- **String to Array Conversion:** When a string is treated as an array, PHP automatically splits the string into individual characters or substrings, creating an array with each character or substring as an element.

```
$colors = "red,green,blue"; // String
$colorArray = explode(",", $colors); // The string will be converted
to an array print_r($colorArray);
/* Output:
Array
(
[0] => red
[1] => green
[2] => blue
)
*/
```

It is important to note that while type juggling can be convenient, it can also introduce potential bugs and confusion in code. It is generally recommended to use explicit type conversions or type-checking functions to ensure the desired behavior and avoid unexpected results.

Type casting

Type casting in PHP refers to the explicit conversion of a value from one data type to another. PHP provides several built-in functions and language constructs for type-casting. Here are the most common type casting operations in PHP:

- **Implicit type casting**: PHP performs implicit type casting automatically in certain situations. For example, adding a string and an integer together results in an implicit conversion of the string to an integer.
- **Explicit type casting**: PHP provides explicit type casting methods using the following constructs:
    - **`(int)` or `(integer)`:** Converts a value to an integer.

    ```
    $number = 3.14;
    $integerNumber = (int)$number; // Explicitly cast to integer
    echo $integerNumber; // Output: 3
    ```

    - **`(float)` or `(double)`:** Converts a value to a floating-point number.

    ```
    $number = 3;
    $floatNumber = (float)$number; // Explicitly cast to float
    echo $floatNumber; // Output: 3.0
    ```

- **(string)**: Converts a value to a string.

```
$number = 10;
$stringNumber = (string)$number; // Explicitly cast to string
echo $stringNumber; // Output: "10"
```

- **(bool)** or **(boolean)**: Converts a value to a boolean.

```
$number = 0;
$booleanValue = (bool)$number; // Explicitly cast to boolean
var_dump($booleanValue); // Output: bool(false)
```

- **(array)**: Converts a value to an array.

```
$number = 5;
$arrayValue = (array)$number; // Explicitly cast to array
print_r($arrayValue);
/*
Output:
Array
(
[0] => 5
)
*/
```

- **(object)**: Converts a value to an object.

```
$data = "Hello";
$objectValue = (object)$data; // Explicitly cast to object
echo $objectValue->scalar; // Output: Hello
```

It is important to note that explicit type casting may lead to unexpected results if the original value cannot be accurately converted to the target type. It is always a good practice to validate and sanitize data before performing type casting to ensure the desired behavior and avoid potential errors.

Operators and expressions

PHP supports various types of **operators** that allow you to perform operations on variables, values, and expressions. Here are the different types of operators in PHP:

- Arithmetic operators:

- Addition: `$a + $b`
- Subtraction: `$a - $b`
- Multiplication: `$a * $b`
- Division: `$a / $b`
- Modulus (Remainder): `$a % $b`
- Exponentiation: `$a ** $b`
- Increment: `++$a or $a++`
- Decrement: `--$a or $a--`

- Assignment operators:
  - Assignment: `$a = $b`
  - Addition assignment: `$a += $b` (equivalent to `$a = $a + $b`)
  - Subtraction assignment: `$a -= $b` (equivalent to `$a = $a - $b`)
  - Multiplication assignment: `$a *= $b` (equivalent to `$a = $a * $b`)
  - Division assignment: `$a /= $b` (equivalent to `$a = $a / $b`)
  - Modulus assignment: `$a %= $b` (equivalent to `$a = $a % $b`)
- Comparison operators:
  - Equal to: `$a == $b`
  - Identical to: `$a === $b`
  - Not equal to: `$a != $b` or `$a <> $b`
  - Not identical to: `$a !== $b`
  - Greater than: `$a > $b`
  - Less than: `$a < $b`
  - Greater than or equal to: `$a >= $b`
  - Less than or equal to: `$a <= $b`
- Logical operators:
  - And: `$a && $b` or `$a and $b`
  - Or: `$a || $b` or `$a or $b`
  - Not: `!$a` or `not $a`
- String operators:
  - Concatenation: `$a . $b`

- Array operators:
    - Union: **`$a + $b`**
    - Equality: **`$a == $b`**
    - Identity: **`$a === $b`**
    - Inequality: **`$a != $b`** or **`$a <> $b`**
    - Non-identity: **`$a !== $b`**
- Conditional operator:
    - Ternary operator: **`$condition ? $valueIfTrue : $valueIfFalse`**
- Type operators:
    - Type equality: **`$a == $b`**
    - Type identity: **`$a === $b`**
    - Instance of: **`$obj instanceof MyClass`**

These are the most commonly used operators in PHP. They enable you to perform mathematical calculations, assign values, compare values, concatenate strings, work with arrays, and make logical decisions in your code.

In PHP, **expressions** are combinations of variables, values, operators, and functions that evaluate a single value. Expressions can be used in assignments, comparisons, calculations, conditions, and many other contexts in PHP. Here are some examples of expressions in PHP:

- Arithmetic expressions

```
$result = 2 + 3 * 4;  // Evaluates to 14

$total = $price * $quantity;  // Evaluates to the product of $price and $quantity
```

- Comparison expressions

```
$isGreater = $a > $b;  // Evaluates to true or false depending on whether $a is greater than $b

$isEqual = $x == $y;  // Evaluates to true or false depending on whether $x is equal to $y
```

- String concatenation expressions

```
$greeting = "Hello, " . $name;  // Concatenates the string "Hello, " with the value of $name
```

- Function call expressions

  ```
  $length = strlen($text);  // Calls the strlen() function to get the length of $text
  ```

- Conditional expressions

  ```
  $maxValue = ($a > $b) ? $a : $b;  // Evaluates to $a if $a is greater than $b; otherwise, it evaluates to $b
  ```

- Array expressions

  ```
  $firstElement = $array[0];  // Accesses the first element of the $array
  ```

- Logical expressions

  ```
  $isTrue = ($x > 0) && ($y < 10);  // Evaluates to true if $x is greater than 0 and $y is less than 10
  ```

Expressions can be as simple as a single variable or value or complex combinations involving multiple operators, functions, and variables. They are essential for performing computations, making decisions, and manipulating data in PHP.

Comments in PHP

In PHP, comments add explanatory or descriptive text within the code that is not executed or interpreted as part of the program. They are useful for documenting code, providing instructions, and making the code more understandable for developers. PHP supports two types of comments:

- **Single-line comments:** Single-line comments begin with `//` and continue until the end of the line. They are used to add comments on a single line.

  ```
  // This is a single-line comment

  $variable = 10; // Assigning a value to the variable
  ```

- **Multi-line comments:** Multi-line comments start with `/*` and end with `*/`. They can span multiple lines and are commonly used for longer comments or commenting out blocks of code.

  ```
  /* This is a multi-line comment
  ```

  It can span multiple lines

  ```
  This is useful for longer explanations or commenting out code */

  $variable = 20;
  ```

Comments are ignored by the PHP interpreter and have no impact on the execution of the code. They are solely for human readers to understand the code. It is good practice to add comments to your code to improve its readability, and maintainability, and to provide useful information to other developers who may work with your code in the future.

Control structures

In PHP, control structures control the flow of execution in a program. They allow you to make decisions, repeat actions, and perform different actions based on certain conditions. PHP provides several control structures, as discussed in *Figure 3.2*:

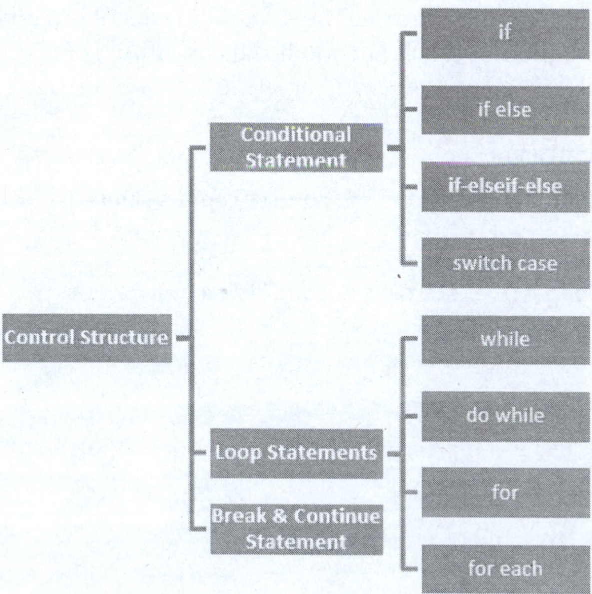

Figure 3.2: Types of control statement

Conditional statements

In PHP, conditional statements are used to make decisions and execute different blocks of code based on certain conditions. PHP provides several conditional statements:

- **`If` statement**: The `if` statement executes a block of code if a condition is true.

  Syntax:

  ```
  if (condition) {
      // Code to execute if condition is true
  }
  ```

Example:

```
$age = 25;

if ($age >= 18) {
    echo "You are an adult.";
}
```

- **`if-else` statement**: The **`if-else`** statement executes a block of code if a condition is true, and another block of code if the condition is false.

  Syntax:

```
if (condition) {
    // Code to execute if condition is true
} else {
    // Code to execute if condition is false
}
```

  Example:

```
$grade = 85;
if ($grade >= 60) {
    echo "You passed the exam.";
} else {
    echo "You failed the exam.";
}
```

- **`if-elseif-else` statement**: The **`if-elseif-else`** statement allows you to test multiple conditions and execute different blocks of code based on the conditions.

  Syntax:

```
if (condition1) {
    // Code to execute if condition1 is true
} elseif (condition2) {
    // Code to execute if condition2 is true
} else {
    // Code to execute if all conditions are false
}
```

Example:

```
$number = 10;

if ($number > 0) {
    echo "Number is positive.";
} elseif ($number < 0) {
    echo "Number is negative.";
} else {
    echo "Number is zero.";
}
```

- **`Switch` statement**: It is used to evaluate an expression and execute different blocks of code based on its value. It provides an alternative way to handle multiple conditions compared to using multiple **if** statements. The syntax of the **switch** statement in PHP is as follows:

  Syntax:

```
switch (expression) {
    case value1:
        // Code to execute if expression equals value1
        break;
    case value2:
        // Code to execute if expression equals value2
        break;
    // Add more cases as needed
    default:
        // Code to execute if expression does not match any case
        break;
}
```

Here is how the **`switch`** statement works:

1. The **`expression`** is evaluated, and its value is compared against the values specified in each **`case`**.
2. If a match is found between the **`expression`** and a **`case`** value, the corresponding block of code is executed. The **`break`** statement is used to exit the **`switch`** statement after the code execution.

3. If no match is found, the code in the **default** block is executed.
4. Optionally, you can omit the **break** statement after each **case** block to allow code execution to 'fall through' to the next **case** block.

   Example:

```
$day = "Monday";
switch ($day) {
    case "Monday":
        echo "It's Monday!";
        break;
    case "Tuesday":
        echo "It's Tuesday!";
        break;
    case "Wednesday":
    case "Thursday":
        echo "It's midweek!";
        break;
    case "Friday":
        echo "It's Friday!";
        break;
    default:
        echo "It's the weekend!";
        break;
}
```

In this example, depending on the value of the **$day** variable, different messages will be printed. If the value is **Monday**, it will print **It's Monday!**. If the value is **Wednesday** or **Thursday**, it will print **It's midweek!**. If none of the case values match the expression, the code in the **default** block will be executed.

The **switch** statement provides a concise way to handle multiple conditions based on the value of an expression, improving code readability and maintainability.

These conditional statements allow you to make decisions in your PHP code based on various conditions. By using conditional statements, you can control the flow of execution and execute different blocks of code based on specific situations or criteria.

Loop statements

In PHP, loop statements allow you to repeat a code block multiple times. They are useful for iterating over arrays, performing calculations, processing data, and executing repetitive tasks. PHP provides several types of loop statements:

- **while** loop: The **while** loop executes a code block as long as a condition is true.

  Syntax:

  ```
  while (condition) { // Code to be executed while the condition is true
  }
  ```

  Example:

  Here is an example of a **while** loop that prompts the user to enter a number until they enter a negative number:

  ```
  echo "Enter a number (enter a negative number to stop): ";
  $number = (int) readline();
  while ($number >= 0) {
      // Perform some operation with the entered number
      echo "You entered: " . $number . "\n";
      // Prompt the user for the next number
      echo "Enter a number (enter a negative number to stop): ";
      $number = (int) readline();
  }
  echo "Loop ended. You entered a negative number.";
  ```

  In this example, the program prompts the user to enter a number. Inside the **while** loop, it performs an operation with the entered number and then prompts the user again for the next number. The loop continues until the user enters a negative number, at which point the loop ends, and a message is displayed.

  This loop allows the user to keep entering numbers until they stop by entering a negative number.

- **do-while loop**: The **do-while** loop is similar to the **while** loop, but it executes the code block at least once before checking the condition.

  Syntax:

  ```
  do { // Code to be executed at least once } while (condition);
  ```

Example:

Here is an example of a **`do-while`** loop in PHP that prompts the user to guess a randomly generated number:

```
$secretNumber = rand(1, 10);
$guess = 0;
do {
    echo "Guess the number (between 1 and 10): ";
    $guess = (int) readline();
    if ($guess > $secretNumber) {
        echo "Too high! Try again.\n";
    } elseif ($guess < $secretNumber) {
        echo "Too low! Try again.\n";
    } else {
         echo "Congratulations! You guessed the correct number: " .
$secretNumber . "\n";
    }
} while ($guess !== $secretNumber);
echo "Game over!";
```

In this example, the program generates a random number between **`1`** and **`10`** and stores it in **`$secretNumber`**. It then prompts the user to guess the number. Inside the **`do-while`** loop, it checks if the user's guess is too high, too low, or the correct number. The loop continues until the user guesses the correct number. Once the correct number is guessed, the loop ends, and a congratulatory message is displayed.

The **`do-while`** loop ensures that the code block is executed at least once before checking the loop condition. It is useful in scenarios where you want to perform an action before checking the condition for repetition.

This example demonstrates the usage of a **`do-while`** loop to create an interactive guessing game.

- **`for`** loop: The **`for`** loop executes a block of code a specific number of times.

  Syntax:

  ```
  for (initialization; condition; increment) { // Code to be executed
  in each iteration }
  ```

Example:

Here is an example of a **for** loop in PHP that prints a multiplication table for a given number:

```
$number = 5;
echo "Multiplication Table for $number:\n";
for ($i = 1; $i <= 10; $i++) {
    $result = $number * $i;
    echo "$number x $i = $result\n";
}
```

In this example, the program sets the value of **$number** to **5**. The **for** loop then iterates from **1** to **10**, with the loop variable **$i** incrementing by **1** in each iteration. Inside the loop, it calculates the multiplication result of **$number** and **$i** and displays the equation and result.

The loop will run 10 times, generating the multiplication table for the number 5. The output will be as follows:

```
Multiplication Table for 5:
5 x 1 = 5
5 x 2 = 10
5 x 3 = 15
5 x 4 = 20
5 x 5 = 25
5 x 6 = 30
5 x 7 = 35
5 x 8 = 40
5 x 9 = 45
5 x 10 = 50
```

This example demonstrates the use of a **for** loop to perform repetitive calculations and display the results in a structured manner.

- **foreach** loop: The **foreach** loop is used to iterate over arrays or other objects.

  Syntax:

  ```
  foreach ($array as $value) { // Code to be executed for each element in the array }
  ```

Example:

```
$fruits = array("Apple", "Banana", "Orange"); foreach ($fruits as
$fruit) { echo $fruit . " "; } // Output: Apple Banana Orange
```

Loop statements allow you to automate repetitive tasks and iterate over data structures in PHP. They provide control over the flow of execution and are essential for handling dynamic data and performing batch operations.

Break and continue statement

In PHP, the break and continue statements are used to control the flow of execution within loops, such as **`for`**, **`foreach`**, **`while`**, and **`do-while`**. They allow you to alter the normal behavior of the loop and control when to exit or skip specific iterations. Here is how each statement works:

- **`break`**: The break statement is used to exit the current loop iteration or terminate the entire loop prematurely. When encountered, the break statement immediately exits the loop and continues with the code execution after the loop.

  ```
  for ($i = 1; $i <= 10; $i++) {
          if ($i === 5) {
                  break; // Exit the loop when $i reaches 5
          }
          echo $i . " ";
  }
  // Output: 1 2 3 4
  ```

  In the example above, when **`$i`** becomes `5`, the **`break`** statement is executed, causing the loop to terminate, and the remaining iterations are skipped.

- **`continue`**: The **`continue`** statement is used to skip the current iteration and move to the next iteration of the loop. When encountered, the continue statement immediately jumps to the next iteration without executing any remaining code within the loop for the current iteration.

  ```
  for ($i = 1; $i <= 5; $i++) {
          if ($i === 3) {
                  continue; // Skip the iteration when $i is 3
          }
          echo $i . " ";
  }
  // Output: 1 2 4 5
  ```

In the example above, when **$i** is equal to **3**, the **continue** statement is executed, causing the loop to skip the code below it and move to the next iteration.

Both **break** and **continue** statements can be used within any loop construct. They provide flexibility and control over the loop execution based on specific conditions.

Functions in PHP

In PHP, functions are blocks of reusable code that perform specific tasks. They allow you to organize your code, improve code reuse, and make your code more modular. PHP supports both built-in functions and user-defined functions. Here is an overview of functions in PHP:

- **Built-in functions:** PHP provides a rich set of built-in functions that perform various operations, such as manipulating strings, working with arrays, performing mathematical calculations, interacting with databases, handling file operations, and more. These functions are readily available and can be used directly in your code without any additional setup or configuration. Examples of built-in functions include **strlen()**, **array_push()**, **date()**, **mysqli_connect()**, and **file_get_contents()**.

- **User-defined functions**: User-defined functions are functions that you create in your PHP code to perform specific tasks. They allow you to encapsulate a code block with a name and parameters, which can be called multiple times throughout your script. User-defined functions are useful for organizing code, improving code readability, and promoting code reuse. You can define a user-defined function using the **function** keyword.

  Syntax:

  ```
  function functionName(parameter1, parameter2, ...) { // Code to be executed }
  ```

  Example:

  ```
  function greet($name) { echo "Hello, " . $name . "!"; } greet("John");
  // Output: Hello, John!
  ```

  User-defined functions can also have optional parameters, default parameter values, and return values.

- **Anonymous functions (Closures):** Anonymous functions, also known as closures, are functions that do not have a specific name. They can be assigned to variables or used directly as function arguments. Anonymous functions are useful when creating a small, inline function without explicitly defining a named function.

  Syntax:

  ```
  $variable = function (parameter1, parameter2, ...) { // Code to be executed };
  ```

Example:

```
$greet = function ($name) { echo "Hello, " . $name . "!"; };
$greet("Alice"); // Output: Hello, Alice!
```

Anonymous functions can capture variables from the surrounding scope, making them useful for creating closures that encapsulate data.

Functions play a fundamental role in PHP development, allowing you to organize and modularize your code, improve code reuse, and encapsulate logic into reusable units. They are an essential component of PHP programming.

Defining PHP function

In PHP, you can define functions to encapsulate reusable blocks of code. Functions allow you to organize your code, improve code reusability, and make your code more modular. Here is the basic syntax for defining a function in PHP:

```
function functionName(parameters) {
// Function body
// Code to be executed when the function is called
// Return statement (optional)
}
```

Let us break down the syntax and explain each part:

- `function`: The keyword used to declare a function in PHP.
- `functionName`: The name you choose for your function. Make sure to follow PHP naming conventions.
- `parameters`: Optional. The variables that the function accepts as input. You can specify zero or more parameters separated by commas.
- `function body`: The block of code enclosed in curly braces `{}` that is executed when the function is called.
- `Return statement`: Optional. If you want your function to return a value, you can use the return statement followed by the value to be returned.

Here is an example of a simple PHP function that calculates the sum of two numbers:

```
function sum($num1, $num2) {
    $result = $num1 + $num2;
    return $result;
}
```

In this example, the function is named **sum** and accepts two parameters **$num1** and **$num2**. It calculates their sum and returns the result using the **return** statement.

To call (or invoke) a function, you simply use its name followed by parentheses () and provide any required arguments:

```
$total = sum(10, 5);
echo $total; // Output: 15
```

In this case, the **sum** function is called with the arguments **10** and **5**, and the returned result is assigned to the variable **$total**, which is then displayed using **echo**.

Calling to function

To call a function in PHP, you need to use the function name followed by parentheses **()**. If the function expects any arguments, you pass them within the parentheses. Here is an example of how to call a function in PHP:

```
// Function definition
function greet($name) {
    echo "Hello, $name!";
}

// Calling the function
greet("John"); // Output: Hello, John!
```

In the example above, we have a function called **greet()** that accepts one parameter **$name**. To call the function, we simply write **greet("John")**, providing the argument **John** within the parentheses.

You can call a function multiple times with different arguments:

```
greet("Alice"); // Output: Hello, Alice!
greet("Bob"); // Output: Hello, Bob!
greet("Emily"); // Output: Hello, Emily!
```

Each time the **greet()** function is called with a different argument, it will execute the code within the function body and produce the corresponding output.

It is important to note that the function you want to call must be defined before you call it in your code. PHP reads the code from top to bottom, so if you define a function after calling it, PHP will generate an error.

Default parameter

In PHP, you can define default parameter values for function arguments. Default parameters allow you to specify a default value that will be used if the corresponding argument is not provided when calling the function. This provides flexibility and allows for more concise function calls.

To define a default parameter value, you can assign a value to the parameter in the function definition. Here is the syntax:

```
function functionName(parameter = defaultValue) {
        // Function body
        // Code to be executed when the function is called
}
```

Let us see an example of a PHP function with a default parameter:

```
function greet($name = "Guest") {
        echo "Hello, $name!";
}
```

In this example, the **greet()** function has one parameter **$name**, and its default value is set to **Guest**. If the function is called without providing a value for **$name**, the default value will be used. If a value is provided when calling the function, it will override the default value.

Let us see some function calls with and without providing a value for the **$name** parameter:

```
greet(); // Output: Hello, Guest!
greet("John"); // Output: Hello, John!
greet("Alice"); // Output: Hello, Alice!
```

In the first call to **greet()**, since no argument is provided, the default value **Guest** is used. In the second and third calls, the provided arguments **John** and **Alice** override the default value.

It is important to note that when using default parameters, any parameters with default values must come after those without default values in the function's parameter list. For example, this is valid:

```
function example($param1, $param2 = "default") {
        // Function body
}
```

```
But the following is not valid:
function example($param1 = "default", $param2) {
// Function body
}
```

In the above example, the parameter with the default value should come after the parameter without a default value.

Parameter passing to a function

In PHP, you can pass parameters to a function in different ways: by value and by reference. The method of parameter passing determines how the function interacts with the passed arguments and affects the original values. Let us explore each method:

- **Passing by value**: By default, PHP uses the 'pass by value' method for parameter passing. It means that when you pass a parameter to a function, a copy of the value is made, and any changes made to the parameter within the function do not affect the original value outside the function.

  Example:

  ```
  function increment($num) {
          $num++;
          echo "Inside function: $num<br>";
  }
  $count = 5;
  increment($count);
  echo "Outside function: $count<br>";

  // Output:
  // Inside function: 6
  // Outside function: 5
  ```

  In this example, the **`increment()`** function receives the value of **`$count`** as a parameter. Inside the function, the value is incremented, but it does not modify the original value of **`$count`** outside the function.

- **Passing by reference**: PHP allows you to pass parameters by reference using the **&** symbol. When a parameter is passed by reference, any changes made to the parameter within the function will affect the original value outside the function.

Example:

```
function incrementByReference(&$num) {
      $num++;
      echo "Inside function: $num<br>";
}
$count = 5;
incrementByReference($count);
echo "Outside function: $count<br>";

// Output:
// Inside function: 6
// Outside function: 6
```

In this example, the **`incrementByReference()`** function receives **`$count`** as a reference parameter using the **&** symbol. Any changes to **`$num`** inside the function will modify the original value of **`$count`** outside the function.

Passing parameters by value is the default behavior and is suitable in most cases. However, passing parameters by reference can be useful when you want to modify the original value within the function. Note that not all functions support passing by reference, so it is important to check the function's documentation to determine if it accepts reference parameters.

Conclusion

In this chapter, we covered the essential aspects of PHP programming. We discussed variables, constants, and their scope, as well as different data types and how PHP handles type juggling and type casting. We explored operators, expressions, and the importance of comments for code documentation. Control structures like loops and conditionals were introduced, along with the usage of break and continue statements. We also delved into functions, including defining and calling them, understanding default parameters, and the various ways of parameter passing. With this knowledge, you now have a solid foundation to build upon and explore more advanced PHP concepts and techniques. In the next chapter, we will discuss PHP arrays and their various functions.

Points to remember

- Variables and constants are used to store and represent data in PHP.
- Variable scope defines the accessibility and lifespan of variables.

- PHP supports various data types, including integers, floats, strings, Booleans, arrays, and objects.
- Type juggling refers to the automatic conversion of variables from one type to another by the PHP interpreter.
- Type casting allows explicit conversion of variables from one type to another, using casting operators.
- Operators and expressions are used for performing calculations, comparisons, and logical operations.
- Comments in PHP are used to add explanatory notes or disable code execution temporarily.
- Control structures like loops and conditionals enable you to control the flow of execution in your code.
- Break and continue statements modify the behavior of loops, allowing you to exit or skip iterations.
- Functions are reusable blocks of code that perform specific tasks.
- Defining a PHP function involves specifying its name, parameters, and the code to be executed.
- Functions are called by using their name followed by parentheses, and arguments can be passed to them.
- Default parameters can be assigned values that are used when no argument is provided for a parameter.
- Parameter passing determines how arguments are transferred to functions, either by value or by reference.

Join our book's Discord space

Join the book's Discord Workspace for Latest updates, Offers, Tech happenings around the world, New Release and Sessions with the Authors:

https://discord.bpbonline.com

Chapter 4
PHP Arrays

Introduction

PHP arrays are essential data structures that store and organize multiple data elements under a single variable name. Arrays in PHP can hold various data types, such as numbers, strings, or even other arrays, making them highly versatile.

To create an array, you use square brackets ([]), and each element in the array is associated with a unique index, starting from zero. The index allows you to access individual elements within the array easily.

PHP arrays can be of two types: indexed arrays and associative arrays. Indexed arrays have numeric keys starting from zero, while associative arrays use custom keys that can be strings or integers. Associative arrays are particularly useful when associating specific values with specific keys, making them more readable and self-descriptive.

Arrays in PHP can grow dynamically, meaning you can add or remove elements as needed during the execution of the script. This flexibility makes arrays a powerful tool for handling data in various scenarios, such as storing user information, managing database records, or processing form inputs.

This chapter will explore how to create, manipulate, and access elements within PHP arrays, enabling you to effectively utilize this fundamental data structure in your PHP applications.

Structure

The chapter covers the following topics:

- Arrays in PHP
- Array functions
- Sorting in PHP
- Functions for extracting data from array
- Adding and removing elements of array
- Shifting elements of an array
- Reversing arrays

Objectives

This chapter aims to provide a comprehensive understanding of arrays in PHP and various array-related functions. Arrays are essential data structures in programming that allow us to store multiple values under a single variable. In this chapter, we will explore how to work with arrays, including functions for creating, manipulating, and extracting data from arrays. We will delve into the array functions available in PHP, which can be used for tasks like sorting elements, adding or removing elements, shifting elements, and reversing the order of arrays. By the end of this chapter, readers will gain proficiency in handling arrays effectively and learn to utilize the array functions to manage and process data in their PHP programs efficiently.

Arrays in PHP

In PHP, arrays are versatile data structures that allow you to store and manage multiple values under a single variable. Arrays can hold various types of data, including numbers, strings, objects, or even other arrays. They are a fundamental tool for organizing and processing data in PHP applications.

There are three primary types of arrays in PHP:

Indexed arrays

These arrays use numeric keys to access elements. The index starts from 0 and increments by 1 for each element. For example:

```
$fruits = array("apple", "banana", "orange");
```

You can access elements using their numeric index:

```
echo $fruits[0]; // Output: "apple"
```

Following is an example of an indexed array in PHP:

```
$colors = array("Red", "Green", "Blue", "Yellow", "Purple");
// Accessing elements by index
echo $colors[0]; // Output: "Red"
echo $colors[2]; // Output: "Blue"
// Modifying an element
$colors[1] = "Cyan";
echo $colors[1]; // Output: "Cyan"
// Adding a new element
 $colors[] = "Magenta";
echo $colors[5]; // Output: "Magenta"
// Length of the array
$length = count($colors);
echo $length; // Output: 6
```

In this example, we created an indexed array called **$colors**, containing five elements representing different colors. We accessed elements using their numeric indices (starting from 0) and modified an element by assigning a new value to it. We also added a new element to the array using the empty square brackets []. Finally, we used the **count()** function to determine the length of the array, which is 6 in this case.

Let us create an indexed array of fruits in PHP:

```
// Indexed array of fruits
$fruits = array("Apple", "Banana", "Orange", "Grapes", "Mango");
// Accessing elements by index
echo "The first fruit in the array is: " . $fruits[0]; // Output: "The first fruit in the array is: Apple"
echo "The third fruit in the array is: " . $fruits[2]; // Output: "The third fruit in the array is: Orange"
// Adding a new fruit to the array
$fruits[] = "Pineapple";
// Length of the array
$length = count($fruits);
echo "The total number of fruits in the array is: " . $length;
// Output: "The total number of fruits in the array is: 6"
```

Process to add a new element to an indexed array in PHP

To add a new element to an indexed array in PHP, you can simply use the empty square brackets [] with no index specified. The new element will be added to the end of the array. In the example above, we added **`Pineapple`** to the **`$fruits`** array using **`$fruits[] = Pineapple`**;

Associative arrays

These arrays use custom keys (strings or integers) to access elements. Each key is associated with a specific value. For example:

```
$person = array("name" => "John", "age" => 30, "country" => "USA");
```

You can access elements using their keys:

```
echo $person["name"]; // Output: "John"
```

Example of associative array in PHP.

```
// Associative array of student information
$student = array(
    "name" => "John Doe",
    "age" => 25,
    "gender" => "Male",
    "email" => "john.doe@example.com",
    "course" => "Computer Science"
);
// Accessing elements by keys
echo "Student Name: " . $student["name"]; // Output: "Student Name: John Doe"
echo "Age: " . $student["age"]; // Output: "Age: 25"
echo "Course: " . $student["course"]; // Output: "Course: Computer Science"
// Modifying an element
$student["email"] = "john.d@example.com";
echo "Email: " . $student["email"]; // Output: "Email: john.d@example.com"
// Adding a new element
$student["phone"] = "123-456-7890";
// Length of the array
$length = count($student);
echo "Number of elements in the array: " . $length; // Output: "Number of
elements in the array: 6"
```

In this example, we created an associative array called **$student**, which stores information about a student, such as name, age, gender, email, and course. Each element in the array is associated with a specific key, making it easier to access and identify the values. We accessed elements using their keys, modified the email address, and added a new element for the phone number. The **count()** function determines the number of elements in the array, which is 6 in this case.

Let us create an example of an associative array of book details in PHP:

```
// Associative array of book details
$book = array(
    "title" => "The Great Gatsby",
    "author" => "F. Scott Fitzgerald",
    "genre" => "Classic",
    "year" => 1925,
    "publisher" => "Charles Scribner's Sons"
);
// Accessing elements by keys
echo "Book Title: " . $book["title"]; // Output: "Book Title: The Great Gatsby"
echo "Author: " . $book["author"]; // Output: "Author: F. Scott Fitzgerald"
echo "Genre: " . $book["genre"]; // Output: "Genre: Classic"
// Modifying an element
$book["year"] = 2021;
echo "Year: " . $book["year"]; // Output: "Year: 2021"
// Adding a new element
$book["language"] = "English";
// Number of elements in the array
$length = count($book);
echo "Number of elements in the array: " . $length; // Output: "Number of
elements in the array: 6"
```

Process to access elements in an associative array in PHP

In PHP, elements in an associative array are accessed using their specific keys. Each element is associated with a key-value pair, where the key is used to identify and access the corresponding value. To access an element, you use the array variable followed by square brackets containing the key. For example, to access the title of the book in the **$book** array, we use **$book["title"]**, and to access the author's name, we use **$book["author"]**.

Multi-dimensional array

In PHP, you can create multi-dimensional arrays, which are arrays containing other arrays as their elements. This allows you to represent data in a structured way, organizing it into rows and columns or even more complex structures like matrices or nested data.

To create a multi-dimensional array in PHP, you simply nest arrays within arrays. Here is how you can do it:

Two-dimensional array

A two-dimensional array is an array of arrays representing rows and columns of data.

```
// Creating a two-dimensional array
$twoDimArray = array(
    array(1, 2, 3),
    array(4, 5, 6),
    array(7, 8, 9)
);
// Accessing elements in a two-dimensional array
echo $twoDimArray[0][1]; // Output: 2
(Accessing the element in the first row, second column)
```

Three-dimensional array

A three-dimensional array is an array of arrays representing more complex structures.

```
// Creating a three-dimensional array
$threeDimArray = array(
    array(
        array(1, 2),
        array(3, 4)
    ),
    array(
        array(5, 6),
        array(7, 8)
    )
);
// Accessing elements in a three-dimensional array
echo $threeDimArray[1][0][1];
// Output: 6 (Accessing the element in the second 2D array, first row, second column)
```

You can continue nesting arrays to create even higher-dimensional arrays if needed.

Here is an example of how you might use a multi-dimensional array to represent a table of data:

```
// Multi-dimensional array representing a table of data
$tableData = array(
    array('Name', 'Age', 'Country'),
    array('John', 30, 'USA'),
    array('Jane', 25, 'Canada'),
    array('Mike', 28, 'UK')
);
// Accessing elements in the table
echo $tableData[1][0];
// Output: John (Accessing the name in the second row, first column)
```

Multi-dimensional arrays are powerful data structures that can be used for various applications, such as representing matrices, organizing hierarchical data, or handling complex datasets.

Let us create a multidimensional array to represent a quiz with questions and multiple-choice answers:

```
// Multidimensional array representing a quiz with questions and answers
$quiz = array(
    array(
        'question' => 'What is the capital of France?',
        'answers' => array(
            'A' => 'London',
            'B' => 'Paris',
            'C' => 'Berlin',
            'D' => 'Rome'
        ),
        'correct_answer' => 'B'
    ),
    array(
        'question' => 'Which planet is known as the "Red Planet"?',
        'answers' => array(
            'A' => 'Venus',
            'B' => 'Mars',
```

```
            'C' => 'Jupiter',
            'D' => 'Neptune'
        ),
        'correct_answer' => 'B'
    ),
    array(
        'question' => 'Who wrote the play "Romeo and Juliet"?',
        'answers' => array(
            'A' => 'William Shakespeare',
            'B' => 'Mark Twain',
            'C' => 'Jane Austen',
            'D' => 'Charles Dickens'
        ),
        'correct_answer' => 'A'
    )
);
// Function to display a quiz question and its multiple choice answers
function displayQuestion($questionData)
{
    echo $questionData['question'] . PHP_EOL;
    foreach ($questionData['answers'] as $option => $answer) {
        echo "$option) $answer" . PHP_EOL;
    }
}
// Display the quiz questions and answers
foreach ($quiz as $index => $questionData) {
    echo "Question " . ($index + 1) . ":" . PHP_EOL;
    displayQuestion($questionData);
    echo PHP_EOL;
}
```

In this example, we have an array called **`$quiz`**, which contains multiple elements, each representing a question in the quiz. Each question element is an array with keys **`question`**, **`answers`**, and **`correct_answer`**. The **`question`** key stores the question itself as a string, the **`answers`** key stores another array containing the multiple-choice options, and the **`correct_answer`** key stores the correct option (A, B, C, or D).

We also have a function **displayQuestion()** to show a question and its multiple choice answers in a formatted manner.

When you run the code, it will display the quiz questions and their options like this:

1. **What is the capital of France?**
   A) London
   B) Paris
   C) Berlin
   D) Rome
2. **Which planet is known as the "Red Planet"?**
   A) Venus
   B) Mars
   C) Jupiter
   D) Neptune
3. **Who wrote the play "Romeo and Juliet"?**
   A) William Shakespeare
   B) Mark Twain
   C) Jane Austen
   D) Charles Dickens

This is a basic example of using a multidimensional array to represent a quiz. You can expand this concept to create more complex quizzes with various types of questions and answers.

Array functions

PHP provides a variety of built-in array functions that allow you to manipulate arrays efficiently. Here are some of the commonly used array functions in PHP:

- **array():** Create an array.
  ```
  $myArray = array(1, 2, 3, 'apple', 'banana');
  ```
- **count():** Count the number of elements in an array.
  ```
  $size = count($myArray);
  ```
- **array_push():** Add one or more elements to the end of an array.
  ```
  $myArray = array(1, 2, 3);
  array_push($myArray, 4, 5);
  // $myArray will now be array(1, 2, 3, 4, 5)
  ```

- **`array_pop()`**: Remove the last element from an array.

```
$myArray = array(1, 2, 3);
$lastElement = array_pop($myArray); // $lastElement will be 3, $myArray
will be array(1, 2)
```

- **`array_shift()`**: Remove the first element from an array.

```
$myArray = array(1, 2, 3);
$firstElement = array_shift($myArray); // $firstElement will be 1,
$myArray will be array(2, 3)
```

- **`array_unshift()`**: Add one or more elements to the beginning of an array.

```
$myArray = array(2, 3);
array_unshift($myArray, 1);
// $myArray will now be array(1, 2, 3)
```

- **`array_slice()`**:Extract a slice of an array.

```
$myArray = array(1, 2, 3, 4, 5);
$slice = array_slice($myArray, 2, 2);
// $slice will be array(3, 4)
```

- **`array_merge()`**: Merge one or more arrays.

```
$array1 = array(1, 2, 3);
$array2 = array(4, 5, 6);
$mergedArray = array_merge($array1, $array2);
// $mergedArray will be array(1, 2, 3, 4, 5, 6)
```

- **`array_search()`**: Search for a value in an array and return its key.

```
$myArray = array('apple', 'banana', 'orange');
$key = array_search('banana', $myArray); // $key will be 1
```

- **`in_array()`**: Check if a value exists in an array.

```
$myArray = array('apple', 'banana', 'orange');
$exists = in_array('banana', $myArray); // $exists will be true
```

- **`array_key_exists()`**: Check if a key exists in an array.

```
$myArray = array('name' => 'John', 'age' => 30);
$exists = array_key_exists('name', $myArray); // $exists will be true
```

- **`array_unique()`**: Remove duplicate values from an array.

  ```
  $myArray = array(1, 2, 2, 3, 4, 4, 5);
  $uniqueArray = array_unique($myArray);
  // $uniqueArray will be array(1, 2, 3, 4, 5)
  ```

These are just a few of the many array functions available in PHP.

Sorting in PHP

PHP provides several built-in functions for sorting arrays. These functions allow you to sort arrays in ascending or descending order based on their keys or values. Here are some of the common sorting functions in PHP:

- **`sort()`:** Sort an array in ascending order based on its values.

  This function sorts an array in ascending order and reindexes the array numerically.

  ```
  $numbers = array(3, 1, 5, 2, 4);
  sort($numbers);
  // $numbers will be sorted and become array(1, 2, 3, 4, 5)
  ```

- **`rsort()`:** Sort an array in descending order based on its values.

  ```
  $numbers = array(3, 1, 5, 2, 4);
  rsort($numbers);
  // $numbers will be sorted and become array(5, 4, 3, 2, 1)
  ```

- **`asort()`**: Sort an array in ascending order based on its values while maintaining key-value associations.

  ```
  $fruits = array('apple' => 3, 'banana' => 1, 'orange' => 5, 'grape'
  => 2);
  asort($fruits);
  // $fruits will be sorted based on values and become array('banana' =>
  1, 'grape' => 2, 'apple' => 3, 'orange' => 5)
  ```

- **`arsort()`**: Sort an array in descending order based on its values while maintaining key-value associations.

  ```
  $fruits = array('apple' => 3, 'banana' => 1, 'orange' => 5, 'grape'
  => 2);
  arsort($fruits);
  // $fruits will be sorted based on values and become array('orange' =>
  5, 'apple' => 3, 'grape' => 2, 'banana' => 1)
  ```

- **ksort()**: Sort an array in ascending order based on its keys.

  ```
  $fruits = array('banana' => 1, 'grape' => 2, 'apple' => 3, 'orange' => 5);
  ksort($fruits);
  // $fruits will be sorted based on keys and become array('apple' => 3, 'banana' => 1, 'grape' => 2, 'orange' => 5)
  ```

- **krsort()**: Sort an array in descending order based on its keys.

  ```
  $fruits = array('apple' => 3, 'banana' => 1, 'grape' => 2, 'orange' => 5);
  krsort($fruits);
  // $fruits will be sorted based on keys and become array('orange' => 5, 'grape' => 2, 'banana' => 1, 'apple' => 3)
  ```

- **usort()**: Sort an array using a user-defined comparison function.

  ```
  $fruits = array('apple', 'banana', 'orange', 'grape');
  usort($fruits, function ($a, $b) {
  return strlen($a) - strlen($b);
  });
  // $fruits will be sorted based on the length of strings and become array('apple', 'grape', 'banana', 'orange')
  ```

These are some of the main array sorting functions in PHP. Each function serves a specific purpose, and the appropriate one to use depends on your specific requirements, such as whether you need to sort by values, keys, or custom comparison rules. Some of these sorting functions modify the original array, while others create a new sorted array.

Functions for extracting data from array

There are several PHP array functions that allow you to extract data from arrays based on different criteria. Here are some of the most commonly used functions for extracting data from arrays:

implode() and **explode()** functions are used to handle strings in different ways:

- **implode():** This function is used to join elements of an array into a single string. It takes two arguments

  Syntax: **string implode (string $glue , array $pieces)**

  $glue: This is the string used to concatenate the elements of the array together in the final string.

`$pieces:` This is the input array containing the elements that need to be combined into a single string.

Example:

```
$array = array('apple', 'banana', 'orange');
$result = implode(', ', $array); echo $result; // Output: "apple, banana, orange"
```

- **`explode()`**: This function is used to split a string into an array of substrings based on a delimiter. It takes three arguments:

  Syntax: **`array explode ( string $delimiter , string $string [, int $limit = PHP_INT_MAX ] )`**

  `$delimiter:` This is the character or string used to split the input string.

  `$string:` This is the input string that needs to be split into an array.

  `$limit` (optional): If specified, this parameter limits the number of elements in the resulting array. If not provided, **`PHP_INT_MAX`** is used as the default value.

  Example:

  ```
  $string = "apple,banana,orange"; $result = explode(',', $string); print_r($result);  // Output: Array ( [0] => apple [1] => banana [2] => orange )
  ```

  Both **`implode()`** and **`explode()`** functions are quite useful for handling data when converting arrays to strings and vice versa. They are often used when working with databases, parsing CSV files, or any situation where you need to convert between arrays and strings.

- **`array_slice():`** Extract a slice of an array.

  ```
  $fruits = array('apple', 'banana', 'orange', 'grape', 'mango');
  $slice = array_slice($fruits, 1, 3);
  // $slice will be array('banana', 'orange', 'grape')
  ```

- **`array_splice():`** Remove and replace elements from an array:

  ```
  $fruits = array('apple', 'banana', 'orange', 'grape', 'mango');
  $removed = array_splice($fruits, 2, 2);
  // $removed will be array('orange', 'grape')
  // $fruits will be array('apple', 'banana', 'mango')
  ```

- **`array_filter():`** Filter elements of an array using a callback function:

  ```
  $numbers = array(1, 2, 3, 4, 5);
  ```

```
$evenNumbers = array_filter($numbers, function ($value)
{
return $value % 2 === 0;
});
// $evenNumbers will be array(2, 4)
```

- **`array_keys()`:** Return all the keys or a subset of keys from an array:

```
$fruits = array('apple', 'banana', 'orange', 'grape', 'mango');
$keys = array_keys($fruits);
// $keys will be array(0, 1, 2, 3, 4)
```

- **`array_values()`:** Return all the values from an array.

```
$fruits = array('apple', 'banana', 'orange', 'grape', 'mango');
$values = array_values($fruits);
// $values will be array('apple', 'banana', 'orange', 'grape', 'mango')
```

- **`array_column()`:** Return the values from a single column in a multi-dimensional array:

```
$students = array(
    array('name' => 'John', 'age' => 25),
    array('name' => 'Jane', 'age' => 28),
    array('name' => 'Mike', 'age' => 30)
);
$names = array_column($students, 'name');
// $names will be array('John', 'Jane', 'Mike')
```

- **`array_search()`:** Search for a value in an array and return its key.

```
$fruits = array('apple', 'banana', 'orange');
$key = array_search('banana', $fruits); // $key will be 1
```

- **`array_key_exists()`**: Check if a key exists in an array.

```
$person = array('name' => 'John', 'age' => 30);
$exists = array_key_exists('name', $person); // $exists will be true
```

- **`in_array()`:** Check if a value exists in an array.

```
$fruits = array('apple', 'banana', 'orange');
$exists = in_array('banana', $fruits); // $exists will be true
```

These are some of the commonly used functions for extracting data from arrays in PHP. Each function serves a specific purpose, and you can choose the one that best fits your requirements.

Adding and removing elements of array

In PHP, arrays are versatile data structures that allow you to store multiple values in a single variable. You can easily add and remove elements from an array using various functions and methods. Here's an explanation of how to add and remove elements from an array in PHP:

- **Adding elements to an array**
  - Using **array_push()**: The **array_push()** function allows you to add one or more elements to the end of an array. Its syntax is as follows:

    ```
    array_push($array, $element1, $element2, ...);
    ```

    - **$array:** The array to which you want to add elements.
    - **$element1, $element2, ...:** The elements you want to add to the array.

    Example:

    ```
    $fruits = array("apple", "banana", "orange");
    array_push($fruits, "grape", "mango");
    print_r($fruits);
    ```

    Output:

    ```
    Array (
        [0] => apple
        [1] => banana
        [2] => orange
        [3] => grape
        [4] => mango
    )
    ```

  - **Using the square bracket notation**: You can directly assign a new value to a specific index of an array to add elements.

    ```
    $array[index] = $value;
    ```

    Example:

    ```
    $colors = array("red", "green", "blue");
    $colors[3] = "yellow"; print_r($colors);
    ```

Output:

```
Array (
    [0] => red
    [1] => green
    [2] => blue
    [3] => yellow
)
```

- **Removing elements from an array**
  - Using **`unset()`**: The **`unset()`** function allows you to remove a specific element from an array by specifying its index.

    ```
    unset($array[index]);
    ```

    Example:

    ```
    $numbers = array(1, 2, 3, 4, 5);
    unset($numbers[2]); // Remove element at index 2 (value 3)
    print_r($numbers);
    ```

    Output:

    ```
    Array (
        [0] => 1
        [1] => 2
        [3] => 4
        [4] => 5
    )
    ```

  - Using **`array_pop()`**: The **`array_pop()`** function removes the last element from the end of an array and returns it.

    ```
    $last_element = array_pop($array);
    ```

    Example:

    ```
    $stack = array("apple", "banana", "cherry");
    $last_fruit = array_pop($stack);
    print_r($stack);
    echo "Removed fruit: " . $last_fruit;
    ```

Output:

```
Array (
    [0] => apple
    [1] => banana
)
Removed fruit: cherry
```

Remember that when you remove an element from an array, the indexes of subsequent elements are re-indexed accordingly.

Shifting elements of an array

In PHP, `array_shift()` and `array_unshift()` are two useful array functions used to add and remove elements from the beginning of an array. Let us discuss the arrays in detail:

- **`array_shift()`:** The **array_shift()** function removes the first element from an array and returns it. It also reindexes the array after the removal. If the array is empty, it returns **null**.

  Syntax:

  ```
  $first_element = array_shift($array);
  ```

  Example:

  ```
  $colors = array("red", "green", "blue");
  $first_color = array_shift($colors);
  print_r($colors);
  echo "Removed color: " . $first_color;
  ```

  Output:

  ```
  Array (
      [0] => green
      [1] => blue
  )
  Removed color: red
  ```

- **`array_unshift()`**: The **`array_unshift()`** function adds one or more elements to the beginning of an array. It reindexes the array after adding the new elements and returns the new number of elements.

Syntax:

```
$new_count = array_unshift($array, $element1, $element2, ...);
```

- **$array:** The array to which you want to add elements.
- **$element1, $element2, ...**: The elements you want to add to the beginning of the array.

Example:

```
$fruits = array("apple", "banana", "orange");

$new_count = array_unshift($fruits, "grape", "mango");

print_r($fruits); echo "New number of elements: " . $new_count;
```

Output:

```
Array (
        [0] => grape
        [1] => mango
        [2] => apple
        [3] => banana
        [4] => orange
)
New number of elements: 5
```

Note: Both array_shift() and array_unshift() modify the original array directly, and the return value of array_unshift() is the new number of elements in the array after the operation.

Reversing arrays

In PHP, there are several ways to reverse an array. We will talk about the three common methods using built-in functions:

- Using **array_reverse()** function: The **array_reverse()** function reverses the order of elements in an array and returns the new reversed array. The original array remains unchanged.

  Syntax:

  ```
  $reversed_array = array_reverse($array);
  ```

  Example:

  ```
  $numbers = array(1, 2, 3, 4, 5);

  $reversed_numbers = array_reverse($numbers);

  print_r($reversed_numbers);
  ```

Output:

```
Array (
        [0] => 5
        [1] => 4
        [2] => 3
        [3] => 2
        [4] => 1
)
```

- Using **`array_reverse()`** with the preserve keys flag: By default, **`array_reverse()`** reindexes the array with numeric keys starting from zero. If you want to preserve the original keys, you can pass **`true`** as the second argument.

  Syntax:

  ```
  $reversed_array = array_reverse($array, true);
  ```

  Example:

  ```
  $colors = array( "a" => "red", "b" => "green", "c" => "blue", );
  $reversed_colors = array_reverse($colors, true);
  print_r($reversed_colors);
  ```

  Output:

  ```
  Array (
          [c] => blue
          [b] => green
          [a] => red
  )
  ```

- Using a loop to reverse the array in place: You can manually reverse the array using a loop to swap the elements from the beginning to the middle of the array.

  Example:

  ```
  $fruits = array("apple", "banana", "orange", "grape", "mango");
  $length = count($fruits);
  for ($i = 0; $i < $length / 2; $i++)
  {
  $temp = $fruits[$i];
  $fruits[$i] = $fruits[$length - $i - 1];
  ```

```
$fruits[$length - $i - 1] = $temp;
}
print_r($fruits);
```

Output:

```
Array (
        [0] => mango
        [1] => grape
        [2] => orange
        [3] => banana
        [4] => apple
)
```

- **array_flip()** function: **array_flip()** function is used to interchange the keys and values of an array. It creates a new array where the keys of the original array become the values, and the values become the keys. This function is particularly useful when you have an associative array and need to quickly switch the positions of keys and values.

  Syntax:

```
flipped_array = array_flip($array);
```

- **$array:** The array whose keys and values you want to flip.

  Example:

```
$original_array = array(
        "apple" => "red",
        "banana" => "yellow",
        "orange" => "orange",
);
$flipped_array = array_flip($original_array);
print_r($flipped_array);
```

Output:

```
Array (
        [red] => apple
        [yellow] => banana
        [orange] => orange
)
```

Conclusion

The chapter delved into the dynamic world of arrays in PHP, offering a comprehensive understanding of their functionality. From the fundamentals of array creation and manipulation to exploring a range of array functions, including sorting, data extraction, and element management, readers have gained a solid understanding of array-related operations. The journey through adding, removing, shifting, and reversing elements in arrays has provided invaluable insights into efficient data handling. After going through this chapter, readers are now equipped to connect the power of arrays effectively, optimizing their code for greater efficiency and readability. As arrays constitute a fundamental building block in PHP programming, mastering these array-related concepts lays a strong foundation for their continued exploration of PHP's capabilities. In the next chapter, readers will learn how to create forms and the process of taking input from the user.

Points to remember

- **Array declaration and initialization**: Arrays in PHP can be declared and initialized using square brackets **`[]`** or the **`array()`** function.
- **Accessing array elements**: Array elements can be accessed using their corresponding index (for indexed arrays) or key (for associative arrays).
- **Array functions**: PHP provides numerous built-in functions for working with arrays, such as **`count()`**, **`in_array()`**, **`array_key_exists()`**, **`array_merge()`**, **`array_push()`**, **`array_pop()`**, **`array_shift()`**, **`array_unshift()`**, and more. Familiarize yourself with these functions to manipulate arrays effectively.
- **Sorting arrays**: PHP offers sorting functions like **`sort()`**, **`rsort()`**, **`asort()`**, **`ksort()`**, **`arsort()`**, **`krsort()`**, and more. These functions allow you to sort arrays in ascending or descending order based on keys or values.
- **Extracting data from arrays**: Functions like **`array_slice()`** and **`array_splice()`** help in extracting specific portions of an array based on the desired start and end positions. Make sure to understand the differences between these functions and how to use them appropriately.
- **Adding and removing elements**: You can add elements to the end of an array using **`array_push()`** or **`array_merge()`**, and remove elements from the beginning using **`array_shift()`** or from the end using **`array_pop()`**. To insert or remove elements at specific positions, use **`array_splice()`**.
- **Shifting elements**: The **`array_shift()`** function allows you to remove the first element of an array and re-index the remaining elements. Conversely, **`array_unshift()`** adds one or more elements to the beginning of an array and adjusts the indices accordingly.

- **Reversing arrays**: Use `array_reverse()` to reverse the order of elements in an array without affecting the original array.
- **Check array functions' return values**: Many array functions may return false on failure. Always check the return value to avoid unexpected behavior in your code.

Section - II

Web Development with PHP

Chapter 5
PHP Forms and User Input

Introduction

In the field of web development, creating dynamic and user-friendly web forms is an essential skill. This chapter explores the world of GUI components, empowering you to design engaging webpages that interact seamlessly with users. You will explore the key concepts and techniques that underpin effective form development using PHP.

The chapter commences with an exploration of GUI components, unraveling the art of crafting visually appealing webpages that engage users through intuitive interfaces. You will uncover the power of forms in PHP, understanding their role in collecting user data and delivering personalized experiences. Both the GET and POST methods are demystified, offering insights into how data is transmitted between clients and servers.

As you progress, you will grab the interesting challenge of embedding multiple forms within a single webpage, mastering the art of optimizing user interaction. Building upon this foundation, the chapter takes a holistic approach to webpage validation, emphasizing the significance of user-friendly error messages and data integrity.

In the realm of user input validation, you will uncover techniques for sanitizing and validating data, fortifying your applications against potential security vulnerabilities. Connecting the synergy of PHP, you will decode the intricacies of processing form data, transforming raw input into meaningful actions.

No exploration of web forms would be complete without knowing cookies and sessions. You will get to know the power of cookies in personalizing user experiences and uncover the potency of sessions in maintaining state across web interactions.

By the chapter's end, you will exercise a robust toolkit to create interactive web forms using PHP, proficiently navigating GUI design, form submission, validation, and data processing. Equipped with this knowledge, you will be prepared to craft user-centric web experiences that seamlessly integrate data interaction, validation, and state management.

Structure

The chapter covers the following topics:

- Creating webpage using GUI components
- Form in PHP
- Submitting form data in PHP using GET() & POST()
- Multiple forms in a single webpage
- Webpage validation
- Validating user input
- Processing form data with PHP
- Cookies in PHP
- Session in PHP

Objectives

This chapter equips you with the knowledge and skills to create captivating webpages enriched with **Graphical User Interface (GUI)** components. The chapter covers the fundamentals of form creation in PHP, including the submission of form data using both `GET()` and `POST()` methods. It explores the implementation of multiple forms within a single webpage and explores the crucial aspects of the webpage and user input validation. The chapter also guides readers through the process of handling form data using PHP, introducing concepts such as cookies and sessions to enhance user interactions and data perseverance. By the end of this chapter, readers will have gained practical insights into building dynamic and interactive web pages with PHP.

Creating a webpage using GUI components

Creating a webpage using GUI components involves designing and structuring a user interface using graphical elements to enhance the user experience. Below are the steps on how to create a webpage using GUI components:

1. **Choose a development environment:** Select a web development environment or framework that supports GUI components. Popular choices include HTML, CSS, and JavaScript libraries like React or Angular.
2. **Design the layout:** Plan the layout of your webpage. Decide on the placement of GUI components such as buttons, input fields, dropdowns, and other interactive elements.
3. **HTML structure:** In your HTML file, create the necessary structure for your webpage. Use HTML tags to define the structure of your GUI components, such as `<div>` for containers, `<button>` for buttons, and `<input>` for input fields.
4. **Common GUI components:** Here are examples of common GUI components you can include on your webpage:
   - **Buttons:** Create buttons using the `<button>` element. Style them with CSS to make them stand out.
   - **Input Fields:** Use the `<input>` element to create text fields, password fields, and more. Apply CSS to define their appearance.
   - **Dropdowns:** Use `<select>` and `<option>` elements to create dropdown menus. JavaScript can be used to handle selected options.
   - **Checkboxes and Radio Buttons:** Use `<input>` with `type="checkbox"` or `type="radio"` to create checkboxes and radio buttons, respectively.
   - **Images:** Insert images using the `<img>` element. Adjust their size and alignment using CSS.
   - **Text Elements:** Use headings (`<h1>` to `<h6>`), paragraphs (`<p>`), and other text-related elements to structure content.
   - **Containers:** Use `<div>` elements to create containers for grouping and styling components.
   - **Navigation:** Create navigation menus using lists (`<ul>` and `<li>`) and style them as desired.
   - **Forms:** Use the `<form>` element to create user input forms. Include input fields, radio buttons, checkboxes, and submit buttons.

Creating webpages using GUI components is about balancing visual design with usability and functionality. By continuously refining your design, you can create a user-friendly and engaging webpage that effectively communicates your content or services.

Form in PHP

In PHP, a form refers to an HTML structure used to collect and submit user input to a web server for processing. Forms are a fundamental part of web applications, enabling users to interact with the application by entering data, making selections, and submitting their inputs for further processing. PHP is commonly used to handle the data submitted through forms and to perform various actions based on that data.

A form in PHP typically consists of HTML form elements, such as input fields, checkboxes, radio buttons, dropdown lists, and buttons. These elements allow users to input different types of data, such as text, numbers, dates, and more. The form is embedded within an HTML **`<form>`** tag, which specifies where the form data should be sent and how it should be sent.

Here is a basic example of an HTML form in PHP:

```
<form action="process.php" method="post">
      <label for="name">Name:</label>
      <input type="text" id="name" name="name" required>
      <br>
      <label for="email">Email:</label>
      <input type="email" id="email" name="email" required>
       <br>
      <input type="submit" value="Submit">
</form>
```

In this example, the form has two input fields (for name and email) and a submit button. The action attribute specifies the PHP file (**`process.php`**) where the form data will be sent for processing. The method attribute is set to "post," indicating that the form data will be sent via the HTTP POST method.

Once the user submits the form, the data entered in the input fields will be sent to the specified PHP file (**`process.php`** in this case). In the PHP file, you can use the **`$_POST superglobal`** to access the submitted form data and perform various actions, such as validation, data processing, and database operations.

A form in PHP is a user interface element used to collect user input, and PHP is used to handle and process the submitted form data on the server side.

Following *Figure 5.1* shows the process of handling forms:

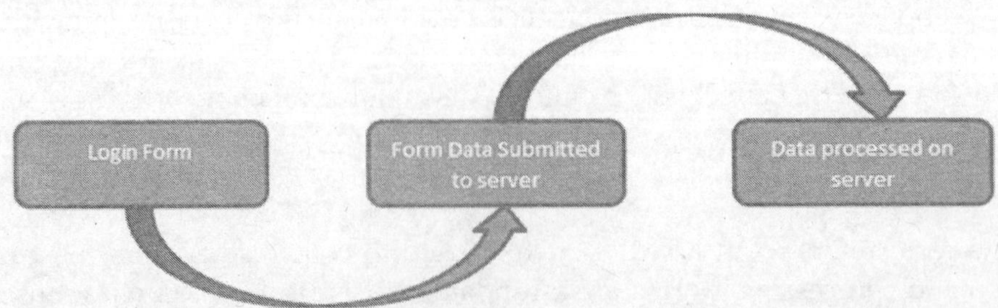

Figure 5.1: *The process of handling form*

Browser and server role in web development

HTML forms in PHP programming run in browsers following these general steps:

1. **Form creation in HTML**: A form (as shown in *Figure 5.2)* is created using HTML tags within the webpage's HTML code. This involves using the **<form>** tag to define the form and its attributes like **action** and **method**. Inside the form, various form elements such as input fields, checkboxes, radio buttons, and buttons are placed.

```
<form action="process.php" method="post">
        <!-- Form elements go here -->
       <input type="text" name="username">
       <input type="password" name="password">
       <input type="submit" value="Submit">
</form>
```

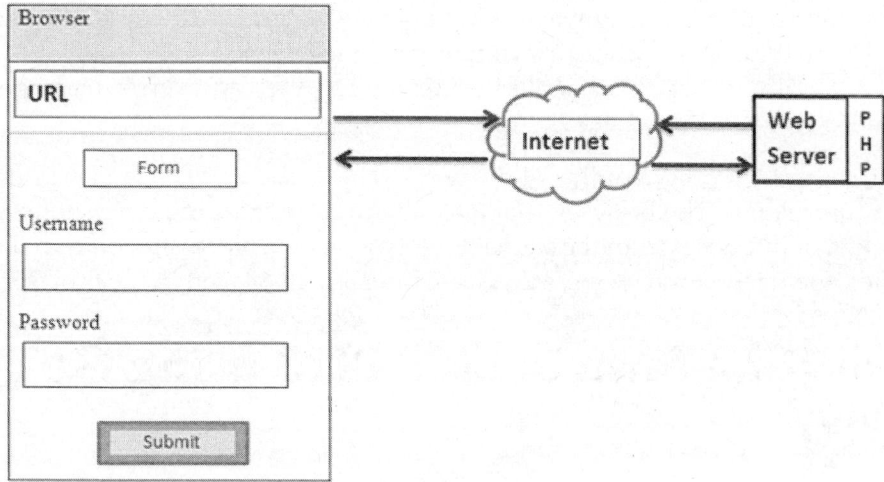

Figure 5.2: Working with HTML forms

2. **User interaction**: When a user interacts with the form by entering data into input fields and clicking the submit button, the browser collects the data and prepares to send it to the server.

3. **Form submission**: Upon clicking the submit button, the browser collects the form data and sends an HTTP request to the URL specified in the action attribute of the **<form>** tag. The HTTP method (GET or POST) is determined by the method attribute.

4. **Server-side processing (PHP):** The server receives the request, and if the action URL points to a PHP file, the PHP script is executed. In the PHP script, you can

access the form data using the **$_POST** or **$_GET** superglobal arrays, depending on the method used.

```
<?php
if ($_SERVER["REQUEST_METHOD"] == "POST") {
        $username = $_POST["username"];
        $password = $_POST["password"];
// Process the data, perform validation, and more
}
?>
```

5. **Server response:** The PHP script can perform various actions based on the form data, such as validating inputs, processing data, interacting with databases, or sending emails. The PHP script generates an appropriate response, which can be HTML content, JSON data, or any other type of output.

6. **Response display in browser:** The response generated by the PHP script is sent back to the browser. The browser interprets the response and displays the resulting content to the user. This could include success messages, error messages, or any other relevant information.

HTML forms in PHP programming allow users to input data, which is then sent to a PHP script for processing. The browser facilitates the form interaction, data submission, and presentation of responses from the server. PHP handles the processing of form data on the server side and generates responses that are ultimately displayed in the browser.

Submitting form data in PHP using GET() & POST()

In PHP, you can retrieve form data submitted using both the **GET** and **POST** methods by using the **$_GET** and **$_POST** superglobals, respectively. Here is how you can handle form data using both methods:

- Using the GET method:

  When you use the GET method in your HTML form, the form data is appended to the URL as query parameters. Here is an example of how to retrieve and process GET method form data in PHP:

  - HTML Form (**get_form.html**)

```
<form action="process.php" method="get">
        <label for="name">Name:</label>
        <input type="text" name="name" id="name">
```

```
        <br>
        <label for="email">Email:</label>
        <input type="email" name="email" id="email">
        <br>
        <input type="submit" value="Submit">
</form>
```

- PHP Script (**process.php**):

```
<?php
if (isset($_GET["name"]) && isset($_GET["email"])) {
        $name = $_GET["name"];
        $email = $_GET["email"];
        // Process and use the data as needed
}
?>
```

- Using the POST Method

  When you use the **POST** method, form data is sent in the request body, making it more secure for sensitive information. Here is how to handle POST method form data in PHP:

- HTML Form (**post_form.html**):

```
<form action="process.php" method="post">
        <label for="name">Name:</label>
        <input type="text" name="name" id="name">
        <br>
        <label for="email">Email:</label>
        <input type="email" name="email" id="email">
        <br>
        <input type="submit" value="Submit">
</form>
```

- PHP Script (**process.php**):

```
<?php
if ($_SERVER["REQUEST_METHOD"] == "POST" && isset($_POST["name"]) &&
isset($_POST["email"]))
```

```
{
        $name = $_POST["name"];
        $email = $_POST["email"];
        // Process and use the data as needed
}
?>
```

In both cases, the PHP script checks if the form data (**name** and **email** in this example) is set in the appropriate superglobal array (**$_GET** or **$_POST**). Then, you can process and use the data according to your requirements.

Remember to validate and sanitize user inputs before using them to prevent security vulnerabilities. Also, choose the appropriate method (GET or POST) based on the sensitivity of the data being submitted.

Difference between GET() & POST() methods

In web development, GET and POST refer to two different HTTP methods used to communicate between a client (such as a web browser) and a server. These methods are commonly used for transferring data between the client and the server. Here are the key differences between GET and POST:

- Data location:
    - **GET:** Data is appended to the URL as query parameters. This means that the data is visible in the URL itself.
    - **POST:** Data is sent in the body of the HTTP request. It is not directly visible in the URL.
- Data size:
    - **GET:** Limited by the maximum length of URLs that browsers and servers can handle. As a result, it is suitable for smaller amounts of data.
    - **POST:** Can handle larger amounts of data as the data is sent in the request body, which does not have the same length limitations as URLs.
- Security:
    - **GET:** Data is visible in the URL, making it less secure for sensitive information like passwords. It can also be cached by browsers and logged in browser history.
    - **POST:** Data is not directly visible in the URL, providing a higher level of security for sensitive information. It is still important to use HTTPS for both GET and POST requests to ensure data encryption.

- Caching and bookmarking:
    - **GET:** GET requests can be cached by browsers and bookmarked, potentially leading to unintended actions if cached data is used or outdated URLs are bookmarked.
    - **POST:** POST requests are not typically cached by browsers, and they are not bookmarked, reducing the risk of unintended actions due to cached or bookmarked data.
- Idempotence:
    - **GET:** In general, GET requests are considered idempotent, meaning that making the same GET request multiple times should not have side effects.
    - **POST:** POST requests are not guaranteed to be idempotent. They can result in different actions each time they are submitted, especially if they modify data on the server.
- Use cases:
    - **GET:** Typically used for fetching data, displaying information, and navigating between pages. It should not be used for actions that modify server data or state.
    - **POST:** Used for submitting forms, creating new resources, and making changes to server data or state. It is suitable for actions that have side effects.

The choice between using GET and POST depends on the nature of the data you are sending, the security requirements, the intended use, and whether the action is meant to be idempotent. It is important to use the appropriate HTTP method for each specific use case to ensure proper functionality and security in your web applications.

Multiple forms in a single webpage

Handling multiple forms on a single webpage in PHP involves similar principles to handling a single form, but you will need to differentiate between the forms and their submitted data. Handling multiple forms on a single webpage in PHP involves creating distinct HTML forms, each with a unique identifier, and utilizing PHP to process the form data based on the submitted form. Here is how you can manage multiple forms on a single webpage using PHP:

- HTML Structure:

  Create your HTML form elements with unique name attributes to differentiate between different forms and their fields. For example:

```
<form action="process_form.php" method="post">
    <!-- Form 1 -->
```

```
    <label for="name1">Name:</label>
    <input type="text" id="name1" name="name1" required>
    <input type="submit" name="submitForm1" value="Submit Form 1">
</form>

<form action="process_form.php" method="post">
    <!-- Form 2 -->
    <label for="name2">Name:</label>
    <input type="text" id="name2" name="name2" required>
    <input type="submit" name="submitForm2" value="Submit Form 2">
</form>
```

- PHP Script:

  In the PHP script that handles the form submissions (**process_form.php** in this example), you can use conditional statements to check which form was submitted based on the names of the submit buttons. Here is an example:

```
<?php
if ($_SERVER["REQUEST_METHOD"] == "POST") {
    if (isset($_POST["submitForm1"])) {
        // Form 1 was submitted
        $name1 = $_POST["name1"];
        // Process form 1 data...
    } elseif (isset($_POST["submitForm2"])) {
        // Form 2 was submitted
        $name2 = $_POST["name2"];
        // Process form 2 data...
    }
}
?>
```

In this example, the script checks which submit button were clicked and process the data accordingly.

Displaying validation errors

If you are performing validation and want to display errors for each form, you can modify the HTML to display errors specific to each form:

```
<form action="process_form.php" method="post">
    <!-- Form 1 -->
    <label for="name1">Name:</label>
    <input type="text" id="name1" name="name1" required>
    <?php if(isset($form1Errors)) { echo "<p class='error'>$form1Errors</
p>"; } ?>
    <input type="submit" name="submitForm1" value="Submit Form 1">
</form>

<form action="process_form.php" method="post">
    <!-- Form 2 -->
    <label for="name2">Name:</label>
    <input type="text" id="name2" name="name2" required>
    <?php if(isset($form2Errors)) { echo "<p class='error'>$form2Errors</
p>"; } ?>
    <input type="submit" name="submitForm2" value="Submit Form 2">
</form>
```

And in your PHP script, set the relevant error messages based on the form being processed.

Webpage validation

Webpage validation typically refers to validating user input on a webpage to ensure that it meets certain criteria or requirements before it is submitted to a server for further processing. This validation can be done on the client side using JavaScript, but it is also essential to validate data on the server side using PHP to ensure data integrity and security. Here is how you can perform webpage validation in PHP:

Client-side validation (JavaScript)

Client-side validation is done using JavaScript to provide instant feedback to users and prevent them from submitting invalid data. While this can enhance user experience, it's important to note that client-side validation can be bypassed by users who disable JavaScript or manipulate it. You can use JavaScript libraries like jQuery or HTML5 form attributes to implement client-side validation.

Server-side validation (PHP)

Server-side validation is the most crucial form of validation since it's not dependent on client-side scripting and is more secure. Here is how you can implement server-side validation using PHP:

```
<?php
$errors = []; // Initialize an array to store validation errors
if ($_SERVER["REQUEST_METHOD"] == "POST") {
    $name = $_POST["name"];
    $email = $_POST["email"];
    // Validate Name
    if (empty($name)) {
        $errors["name"] = "Name is required.";
    }
    // Validate Email
    if (empty($email)) {
        $errors["email"] = "Email is required.";
    } elseif (!filter_var($email, FILTER_VALIDATE_EMAIL)) {
        $errors["email"] = "Invalid email format.";
    }
    // If no errors, process the data
    if (empty($errors)) {
        // Perform further processing (e.g., database operations)

        // Redirect or display a success message
    }
}
?>
```

In this example, the script validates the name and email fields, checking for both emptiness and valid email format. If validation fails, error messages are stored in the **`$errors`** array. If there are no errors, further processing can be performed.

Displaying validation errors

To display validation errors to users, you can modify your HTML form to show error messages next to the respective fields. For example:

```
<form action="process_form.php" method="post">
    <label for="name">Name:</label>
    <input type="text" id="name" name="name" required>
    <?php if(isset($errors["name"])) { echo "<p
class='error'>{$errors['name']}</p>"; } ?>
    <br>
```

```
    <label for="email">Email:</label>
    <input type="email" id="email" name="email" required>
    <?php if(isset($errors["email"])) { echo "<p
class='error'>{$errors['email']}</p>"; } ?>
    <br>
    <input type="submit" value="Submit">
</form>
```

In this example, if there are errors for the name or email fields, error messages are displayed next to the respective fields.

Validating user input

Validating user input is a crucial step in web development to ensure that the data submitted through forms is accurate, safe, and meets the expected format. In PHP, you can perform input validation using a combination of built-in functions, regular expressions, and custom validation logic. Here is a step-by-step guide on how to validate user input in a PHP form:

1. **Client-side validation:** Implementing client-side validation using JavaScript is a good practice to provide immediate feedback to users. However, it should not be relied upon solely, as malicious users can bypass it.

2. **Server-side validation:** Server-side validation is essential to ensure data integrity and security. Here is how you can perform validation in PHP:

    a. **Sanitize input:** Use `filter_input()` or `filter_var()` functions to sanitize and validate input data. Sanitizing removes any harmful characters or tags from the input.

    ```
    $email = filter_input(INPUT_POST, 'email', FILTER_SANITIZE_EMAIL);
    ```

    b. **Validate required fields:** Check if required fields are present and not empty.

    ```
    if (empty($_POST['username'])) {
        $errors[] = "Username is required.";
    }
    ```

    c. **Validate data format:** Use regular expressions or built-in functions to validate specific data formats like email addresses, URLs, dates, and more.

    ```
    if (!filter_var($email, FILTER_VALIDATE_EMAIL)) {
        $errors[] = "Invalid email format.";
    }
    ```

d. **Validate numeric input:** Ensure numeric input values are valid.

```
$age = filter_input(INPUT_POST, 'age', FILTER_VALIDATE_INT);
        if ($age === false) { $errors[] = "Age must be a valid
number.";
}
```

e. **Custom validation logic:** Implement custom validation rules based on your application's requirements.

```
$password = $_POST['password'];
        if (strlen($password) < 8) { $errors[] = "Password must
be at least 8 characters.";
}
```

f. **Display errors:** If there are validation errors, display them to the user.

```
If (!empty($errors)) {
        foreach ($errors as $error) {
                echo "<p>$error</p>";
        }
}
```

Input validation is just one aspect of web application security. Always use prepared statements or parameterized queries when interacting with databases to prevent SQL injection and consider other security measures like data validation and output encoding to prevent other types of attacks.

Processing form data with PHP

Processing form data with PHP involves retrieving and handling data submitted from an HTML form. Here is a step-by-step guide on how to do this:

1. **Create the HTML Form:**

   Start by creating an HTML form in your web page. The form should have a method (POST or GET) and an action attribute that points to the PHP script that will process the form data. Here is an example of a simple form:

```
<form action="process_form.php" method="post">
         <label for="name">Name:</label>
        <input type="text" id="name" name="name" required>
        <br>
```

```
        <label for="email">Email:</label>
        <input type="email" id="email" name="email" required>
        <br>
        <input type="submit" value="Submit">
</form>
```

2. **Create the PHP Script:**

   Create a PHP script (for example, **`process_form.php`**) that will handle the form data. In this script, you can access the form data using the **`$_POST`** or **`$_GET`** superglobal arrays, depending on the method used in the form.

```
<?php
if ($_SERVER["REQUEST_METHOD"] == "POST") {
        // Retrieve form data
        $name = $_POST["name"];
        $email = $_POST["email"];
        // Process the data (you can perform validation, database
operations, etc.)
        // For now, let's just display the data
        echo "Name: $name<br>";
        echo "Email: $email";
}
?>
```

   In this example, the script first checks if the request method is POST, then it retrieves the **name** and **email** values from the **`$_POST`** array. It then processes and displays the data. You can replace the echo statements with any processing you need to perform, such as saving data to a database or sending emails.

3. **Form data validation:**

   It is important to validate the form data to ensure it's in the expected format and to prevent security issues like SQL injection or **Cross-Site Scripting (XSS)** attacks. You can use PHP's built-in functions like **`filter_var`** and regular expressions for validation.

4. **Sanitization:**

   Sanitize the data to remove any potentially harmful content. For example, you can use the **`htmlspecialchars`** function to prevent XSS attacks when displaying user-generated data on your page.

This is just a basic example. In a real-world scenario, you might want to validate the data more thoroughly, use prepared statements when interacting with databases to prevent SQL injection and handle errors gracefully.

Handling multivalued forms in PHP

Handling multivalued forms in PHP involves processing form submissions where one or more form fields can have multiple values. This is often the case with checkboxes, multiple select lists, or dynamic form fields. Here are the basic steps to handle multivalued forms in PHP:

HTML Form (Example with Checkboxes)

```
<!DOCTYPE html>
<html lang=»en»>
<head>
    <meta charset="UTF-8">
    <meta name="viewport" content="width=device-width, initial-scale=1.0">
    <title>MultiValued Form</title>
</head>
<body>
    <form action="process_form.php" method="post">
        <label for="fruits">Select fruits:</label><br>
        <input type="checkbox" name="fruits[]" value="apple"> Apple<br>
        <input type="checkbox" name="fruits[]" value="banana"> Banana<br>
        <input type="checkbox" name="fruits[]" value="orange"> Orange<br>
        <input type="submit" value="Submit">
    </form>
</body>
</html>
```

PHP Form Processing (process_form.php)

```
<?php
if ($_SERVER["REQUEST_METHOD"] === "POST") {
    // Check if the "fruits" array is set in the form data
    if (isset($_POST["fruits"])) {
        // Access the selected fruits
        $selectedFruits = $_POST["fruits"];

        // Process each selected fruit
```

```
        foreach ($selectedFruits as $fruit) {
            echo "Selected Fruit: " . htmlspecialchars($fruit) . "<br>";
        }
    } else {
        echo "No fruits selected.";
    }
}
?>
```

In this example, the form contains checkboxes with the same name (**fruits[]**) and different values. Using [] in the name attribute allows PHP to treat it as an array when the form is submitted. In the PHP processing script, **$_POST["fruits"]** will be an array containing the selected fruits.

Note:

a) **Check if the Form is Submitted: Use $_SERVER["REQUEST_METHOD"] === "POST" to check if the form has been submitted.**

b) **Use Array Notation in Form Fields: When dealing with multivalued fields, use array notation in the field names (e.g., name="fruits[]") to let PHP treat them as arrays.**

c) **Check if Array is Set: Before accessing the values of multivalued fields in PHP, check if the array is set using isset($_POST["fruits"]) to avoid errors.**

d) **Loop through the Array: Use a loop (e.g., foreach) to process each value in the array.**

By following these steps, you can handle multivalued forms in PHP and process the submitted data accordingly. Adjust the form and processing logic based on the specific requirements of your application.

Cookies in PHP

Cookies in PHP are a way to store small pieces of data on the user's browser, which can be later retrieved and used by the server. Cookies are often used to remember user preferences, session information, and other data that needs to persist across different pages or visits.

Here is how you can work with cookies in PHP:

1. **Setting a cookie**: You can set a cookie using the **setcookie()** function. The basic syntax is:

   ```
   setcookie(name, value, expire, path, domain, secure, httponly);
   ```

It is explained as follows:

- **name:** The name of the cookie.
- **value:** The value to be stored in the cookie.
- **expire:** The expiration time of the cookie (in Unix timestamp format). If not specified, the cookie will expire when the browser is closed.
- **path:** The path on the server for which the cookie will be available. Use '/' to make the cookie available for the entire domain.
- **domain:** The domain for which the cookie is valid. Use '.' followed by the domain name to make it available for subdomains.
- **secure:** If set to true, the cookie will only be transmitted over secure (HTTPS) connections.
- **httponly:** If set to true, the cookie will only be accessible through the HTTP protocol and not by JavaScript.

Example:

```
setcookie("username", "john_doe", time() + 3600, "/", ".example.com",
false, true);
```

2. **Accessing Cookie Values**: Once a cookie is set, you can access its value using the $_COOKIE superglobal array. For example:

```
$username = $_COOKIE["username"];
```

3. **Deleting a Cookie**: To delete a cookie, you can set its expiration time to a time in the past. This effectively makes the browser remove the cookie.

```
setcookie("username", "", time() - 3600, "/");
```

Cookies have limitations such as a maximum size of around 4KB and being susceptible to security vulnerabilities like XSS attacks. It is important to avoid storing sensitive information in cookies and to sanitize and validate user input when dealing with cookies.

Additionally, modern web development often uses alternatives to cookies, such as session management and local storage, for various use cases.

Example to create cookies in PHP

```
<?php
// Set a cookie
$cookie_name = "user";
$cookie_value = "john_doe";
$expiration_time = time() + 3600; // Cookie will expire in 1 hour
```

```
$cookie_path = "/"; // Available for the entire domain
$cookie_domain = ".example.com"; // Available for subdomains
$secure = false; // Not limited to secure (HTTPS) connections
$httponly = true; // Only accessible via HTTP, not JavaScript

setcookie($cookie_name, $cookie_value, $expiration_time, $cookie_path,
$cookie_domain, $secure, $httponly);

// Retrieve and display the cookie value
if(isset($_COOKIE[$cookie_name])) {
    $username = $_COOKIE[$cookie_name];
    echo "Welcome back, $username!";
} else {
    echo "Welcome, guest!";
}
?>
```

In this example, a cookie named "user" is created with the value "**`john_doe`**". It will expire in 1 hour, be available for the entire domain, and be accessible via HTTP only. The cookie's value is then retrieved and displayed on the page. If the cookie does not exist, a default "**`Welcome, guest!`**" message is shown.

Note: You need to replace "example.com" with your actual domain and adapt the cookie name and value to your use case. Also, be cautious when dealing with user-related data and ensure you handle them securely.

Accessing cookies with PHP

Accessing cookies in PHP is straightforward using the **`$_COOKIE`** superglobal array. The **`$_COOKIE`** array contains all the cookies that have been sent by the user's browser to the server. You can access cookie values using the cookie names as keys in this array. Here is an example:

Assuming you have a cookie named "username":

```
<?php
if (isset($_COOKIE["username"])) {
    $username = $_COOKIE["username"];
    echo "Welcome back, $username!";
} else {
    echo "Welcome, guest!";
```

```
}
?>
```

In this example, the code checks if the "username" cookie is set using **`isset($_COOKIE["username"])`**. If the cookie is set, it retrieves the value using **`$_COOKIE["username"]`** and displays a welcome message with the username. If the cookie is not set, it displays a default welcome message for guests.

The cookies are stored as key-value pairs and are sent along with each HTTP request to the server. Always validate and sanitize cookie values before using them in your application to prevent security vulnerabilities.

Check the cookie is set or not

To check if a cookie is set or not in PHP, you can use the **`isset()`** function along with the **`$_COOKIE`** superglobal array. Here is how you can do it:

```
<?php
$cookie_name = "username";
if (isset($_COOKIE[$cookie_name])) {
    $username = $_COOKIE[$cookie_name];
    echo "Welcome back, $username!";
} else {
    echo "Welcome, guest!";
}
?>
```

In this example, the code checks if the cookie named "**`username`**" is set by using **`isset($_COOKIE[$cookie_name])`**. If the cookie is set, it retrieves the value from the **`$_COOKIE`** array and displays a welcome message with the username. If the cookie is not set, it displays a default welcome message for guests.

Note: You need to replace "username" with the actual name of the cookie you want to check. Also, keep in mind that cookies are stored on the user's browser and are sent to the server with each HTTP request, so you can use this method to check the presence of cookies that were set during previous interactions with the user.

Modify and delete cookies values

You can modify and delete cookies in PHP using the **`setcookie()`** function. Here is how you can do that:

Modify a Cookie

To modify a cookie, you can simply use the **setcookie()** function again with the same cookie name. The new value and other parameters will overwrite the existing cookie's value and settings. For example:

```
$cookie_name = "username";
$new_username = "jane_doe";
setcookie($cookie_name, $new_username, time() + 3600, "/");
```

This code will update the value of the "**username**" cookie to "**jane_doe**" and extend its expiration time by 1 hour.

Delete a Cookie

To delete a cookie, you can set its expiration time to a past time. This will prompt the browser to remove the cookie. For example:

```
$cookie_name = "username";
setcookie($cookie_name, "", time() - 3600, "/");
```

In this code, the cookie named "**username**" is set to expire in the past, effectively removing it.

When you modify or delete a cookie, you need to use the same parameters (like **path**, **domain**, **secure**, **httponly**) that were used when the cookie was originally set, so the browser can properly identify the cookie you want to modify or delete.

Following is an example to demonstrate modifying and deleting a cookie:

```
<?php
$cookie_name = "username";
// Check if the cookie is set
if (isset($_COOKIE[$cookie_name])) {
    $username = $_COOKIE[$cookie_name];
    echo "Welcome back, $username!<br>";
} else {
    echo "Welcome, guest!<br>";
}

// Modify the cookie
$new_username = "jane_doe";
setcookie($cookie_name, $new_username, time() + 3600, "/");
```

```
echo "Cookie modified. New value: $new_username<br>";

// Delete the cookie
setcookie($cookie_name, "", time() - 3600, "/");
echo "Cookie deleted.";
?>
```

In this example, the code first checks if the "**username**" cookie is set, then modifies it, and finally deletes it.

Session in PHP

In PHP, sessions are a way to maintain and manage user-specific data across multiple pages and requests. Unlike cookies, which are stored on the user's browser, session data is stored on the server. This makes sessions more secure for sensitive information and larger data sets.

Here is how sessions work in PHP:

Starting a session: To start a session, you use the **session_start()** function. Typically, you place this function at the beginning of your PHP script before any output is sent to the browser. This function initializes the session and allows you to store and retrieve data in the session.

```
<?php
session_start();
// Rest of your code...
?>
```

Storing data in a session: You can store data in a session using the **$_SESSION** superglobal array. This array acts as a container for session variables. For example:

```
<?php
session_start();
$_SESSION["username"] = "john_doe";
$_SESSION["user_id"] = 123;
// Rest of your code...
?>
```

Accessing session data: You can access session data by using the **$_SESSION** superglobal array. For example:

```
<?php
session_start();
if (isset($_SESSION["username"])) {
```

```
        $username = $_SESSION["username"];
        echo "Welcome back, $username!";
} else {
echo "Welcome, guest!"; }
// Rest of your code... ?>
```

Ending a session: When you are done using session data, you can end the session using the **`session_destroy()`** function. This will clear all session data and cookies associated with the session.

```
<?php
session_start();
// Do something with session data...
session_destroy();
?>
```

Sessions provide a convenient way to manage user-specific data throughout their visit on your website. However, they require session management, including handling session timeouts and security considerations.

To work with sessions effectively, you need to ensure that your server is configured to support sessions (usually through PHP's configuration settings) and that the session-handling functions are used appropriately in your code.

Conclusion

Concluding this chapter, you have gained a robust foundation in building compelling web experiences. From GUI components and form creation to validation, user input handling, and data management with PHP, you are equipped to craft interactive and secure web applications. By mastering cookies and sessions, you are prepared to create personalized journeys for users. With these skills in hand, you are poised to create web solutions that seamlessly marry form and function, delivering engaging experiences to users worldwide. Your new expertise lays the groundwork for innovative web projects and further exploration in the ever-evolving world of web development.

Points to remember

- Creating a webpage using GUI components:
  - GUI components enhance user interaction and aesthetics.
- Form in PHP:
  - Forms collect user data and enable user interactions.
  - Use HTML **`<form>`** elements to create forms.

  - PHP is used to handle form submissions and process data.
- Submitting form data using **`GET()`** & **`POST()`**:
  - Use the GET method for simple queries and retrieving data.
  - Use the POST method for secure and complex data submissions.
  - Data is sent as URL parameters with GET and in the request body with POST.
- Multiple forms in a single webpage:
  - Embedding multiple forms improves user flow and organization.
  - Assign unique form names and action URLs for each form.
  - Use hidden fields or JavaScript to manage form interactions.
- Webpage validation:
  - Validate user inputs on both client-side (JavaScript) and server-side (PHP).
  - Display clear error messages to guide users.
  - Validate data types, lengths, and formats.
- Validating user input:
  - Protect your application against security threats like SQL injection and XSS.
  - Sanitize and validate user inputs to prevent malicious data from entering your system.
- Processing form data with PHP:
  - Use PHP to access form data using the **`$_POST`** or **`$_GET`** superglobals.
  - Process and sanitize data before using it in your application.
  - Perform actions based on form inputs, like database updates or sending emails.
- Cookies in PHP:
  - Cookies store small data on the user's browser.
  - Use cookies to remember user preferences or maintain user sessions.
  - Set and retrieve cookies using the **`setcookie()`** function and **`$_COOKIE`** superglobal.
- Session in PHP:
  - Sessions store data on the server and maintain user state.
  - Use **`session_start()`** to initiate a session.
  - Store and retrieve session data using the **`$_SESSION`** superglobal.
  - Destroy sessions when no longer needed with **`session_destroy()`**.

CHAPTER 6
PHP Strings

Introduction

In the realm of web development, the art of crafting dynamic and engaging web applications often begins with strings – those sequences of characters that form the lifeblood of textual content. PHP, a versatile and widely used scripting language, empowers developers with a rich set of tools to connect the potential of strings. This chapter is your gateway into the world of PHP strings and functions, where we will delve into the fundamental concepts and practical techniques for working with text. From the basics of creating and manipulating strings to exploring string functions, this chapter will equip you with the knowledge and skills necessary to employ the power of strings effectively in your PHP web development endeavors. Whether you are just starting your journey in PHP or seeking to deepen your understanding, this chapter will serve as your essential guide to mastering the art of string manipulation in PHP.

Structure

The chapter covers the following topics:

- Creating and manipulating strings
- Types of string in PHP
- PHP strings

- Escape sequences in PHP
- String functions
- Printing strings in PHP
- Comparing strings

Objectives

The objective of this chapter is to provide a comprehensive understanding of PHP strings and the functions associated with them. We aim to equip you with the knowledge and practical skills necessary to work effectively with textual data in PHP. By the end of this chapter, you will have a solid grasp of how to create, manipulate, and utilize strings in PHP, as well as a deep dive into the array of built-in string functions that PHP offers. Whether you are a beginner looking to establish a strong foundation in PHP or an experienced developer seeking to enhance your string-handling abilities, this chapter will guide you to becoming proficient in the art of string manipulation and empower you to create dynamic and interactive web applications with confidence.

Creating and manipulating strings

In PHP, a string is a sequence of characters that can be used to store and manipulate textual data. Strings are one of the fundamental data types in PHP and are widely used in web development for tasks like handling user input, generating HTML content, working with databases, and more. PHP strings are fundamental data types and are used extensively for various tasks. Here is how you can create and manipulate strings in PHP:

String declaration

You can declare/create a string in PHP using single quotes (') or double quotes ("). For example:

```
$singleQuotedString = 'This is a single-quoted string.';

$doubleQuotedString = "This is a double-quoted string.";
```

Double-quoted strings offer more features, like variable interpolation and escape sequences (for example, \n for newline), while single-quoted strings are more straightforward and do not interpolate variables or interpret escape sequences.

Concatenation

String concatenation is done using the . operator:

```
$string1 = "Hello";

$string2 = "World";
```

```
$result = $string1 . " " . $string2;
// concatenating with a space in between echo $result;
// Output: "Hello World"
```

Accessing characters

PHP strings are zero-indexed, meaning you can access individual characters using square brackets:

```
$str = "Hello, world!";
$firstChar = $str[0]; // $firstChar will be 'H'
```

Substring extraction

You can extract a portion of a string using the **substr()** function:

```
$str = "Hello, world!";
$substring = substr($str, 0, 5); // $substring will be "Hello"
```

String interpolation

In PHP, you can directly embed variables in double-quoted strings:

```
$name = "Alice";
$age = 30;
$greeting = "My name is $name and I am $age years old.";
echo $greeting;
// Output: "My name is Alice and I am 30 years old."
```

String functions

PHP offers a variety of built-in string functions for manipulation:

```
$text = "PHP Programming ";
echo trim($text); // Removes leading and trailing spaces
echo strtolower($text); // Converts to lowercase
echo strtoupper($text); // Converts to uppercase
echo str_replace("P", "C", $text); // Replaces "P" with "C"
echo strpos($text, "Programming"); // Finds the position of "Programming"
```

String length

You can find the length of a string using the **strlen()** function:

```
$text = "Hello, world!";
$length = strlen($text);
echo $length;
// Output: 13
```

String indexing and slicing

You can access individual characters or substrings using indexes:

```
$text = "PHP";
echo $text[0]; // Output: "P"
echo substr($text, 1, 2); // Output: "HP" (starting from index 1, 2
characters)
```

Escape sequences

PHP supports escape sequences within strings, similar to other programming languages:

```
$escaped_string = "This is a \"quote\" in a string.";
$line_break = "This is a line break:\nSecond line.";
```

These are just some of the basic operations for creating and manipulating strings in PHP. The language provides a rich set of string functions and methods for more advanced string manipulation tasks as well.

Types of strings

In PHP, strings are sequences of characters and can be represented in various ways. Here are the types of strings in PHP:

- **Single-quoted strings:** In the context of PHP, single-quoted strings are encapsulated within single quotation marks (' '). One key characteristic of these single-quoted strings is that any variables included within them are not expanded or replaced with their values; they are interpreted entirely literally. This means that the variable names themselves will be treated as plain text, preserving their original form.

  Additionally, PHP's single-quoted strings do support a limited set of escape sequences, such as '\', which represents a literal backslash, and '\' to represent a single quotation mark within the string. However, it is essential to note that, unlike double-quoted strings in PHP, single-quoted strings do not recognize most escape sequences or variables. This feature makes single-quoted strings valuable when you need to maintain the exact textual content without any variable substitution or extensive escape sequence interpretation in PHP code.

  Example:

  ```
  $str = 'This is a single-quoted string';
  ```

- **Double-quoted strings:** In PHP, double-quoted strings are defined within double quotation marks (" "). These strings possess distinct characteristics that set them apart. One notable feature is that variables enclosed within double-quoted strings are automatically expanded, meaning their values are included directly within the string. This allows for dynamic content incorporation, making it convenient for displaying variable values within text.

  Moreover, double-quoted strings in PHP also process various escape sequences, including "" to represent a double quotation mark, '\\' for a literal backslash, '\n' for a newline, '\r' for a carriage return, and many others. These escape sequences are interpreted and replaced with their corresponding characters when the string is evaluated.

  In summary, double-quoted strings in PHP provide the flexibility of variable interpolation, where variables are expanded to their values, along with the convenience of processing escape sequences, making them a versatile choice for constructing strings with dynamic content and special character handling.

  Example:

  ```
  $name = "John";
  $str = "Hello, $name!";
  ```

- **Heredoc**: Heredoc is a convenient mechanism in PHP for creating multiline strings. The syntax begins with <<< followed by an identifier of your choice and concludes with the same identifier. One notable feature of heredoc is its ability to expand variables within the string, allowing for dynamic content inclusion. This makes heredoc an efficient and readable solution for handling large blocks of text or HTML in PHP, enhancing code clarity and maintainability.

  Example:

  ```
  $text = <<<EOT
  This is a heredoc string.
  It can span multiple lines.
  Variables like \$name are expanded: $name
  EOT;
  ```

- **Nowdoc:** Similar to heredoc, nowdoc provides a method for creating multiline strings in PHP; however, it is enclosed in single quotes (' ') instead of double quotes. Especially, nowdoc strings differ from heredoc in that variables within them are not expanded; they are interpreted literally. This makes nowdoc particularly useful when you want to preserve the exact content, including the representation of variables, without any parsing or interpretation within the string. Nowdoc offers a straightforward way to handle static or unaltered textual data in your PHP code.

Example:

```
$text = <<<'EOT'
This is a nowdoc string.
Variables like \$name are not expanded: $name
EOT;
```

- **Concatenation**: Strings can be concatenated using the " . "operator.

  Example:

  ```
  $str1 = "Hello, ";
  $str2 = "world!";
  $result = $str1 . $str2;
  ```

- **String interpolation (PHP 5.5+):** You can also use string interpolation with double-quoted strings using {} to enclose variables.

  Example:

  ```
  $name = "Alice";
  $str = "Hello, {$name}!";
  ```

These are the main types of strings in PHP. The choice of which one to use depends on specific requirements for string manipulation, variable interpolation, and readability.

Escape sequences in PHP

Escape sequences in PHP are special character sequences used within strings to represent characters that are difficult to include directly in a string. These sequences begin with a backslash \ followed by a character that defines the escape sequence. *Table 6.1* depicts some common escape sequences in PHP:

\\: Backslash	Represents a literal backslash.
\': Single Quote	Represents a single quote character within a single-quoted string.
\": Double Quote	Represents a double quote character within a double-quoted string.
\n: Newline	Represents a newline character, commonly used for line breaks.
\r: Carriage Return	Represents a carriage return character, used in some systems to move the cursor to the beginning of the line.
\t: Tab	Represents a tab character, used to create horizontal whitespace.
\v: Vertical Tab	Represents a vertical tab character.

Table 6.1: *Common Escape Sequences in PHP*

These escape sequences are useful when you need to include special characters or control characters within your PHP strings. They are particularly important when working with text formatting, file input/output, and other situations where you need to represent characters that cannot be typed directly or might be misinterpreted by PHP.

Example usage:

```
$escaped = "This is a single-quoted string with a newline:\nAnd a tab:\t";
$doubleQuoted = "This is a double-quoted string with a variable: \$variable";
```

String functions

PHP offers various functions and features for working with strings. PHP provides a wide range of built-in functions for string manipulation, such as **str_replace()**, **strpos()**, **str_split()**, **strtolower()**, **strtoupper()**, and many more. These functions make it easy to perform common operations on strings.

Here are some commonly used string functions in PHP:

- **strtolower($string)** and **strtoupper($string)**: Convert a string to lowercase or uppercase.

  ```
  $text = "Php Programming";
  $lower = strtolower($text);
  // $lower will be "php programming"
  $upper = strtoupper($text);
  // $upper will be "PHP PROGRAMMING"
  ```

- **trim($string)**: Removes leading and trailing whitespace or specified characters from a string.

  ```
  $text = " Trim this ";
  $trimmed = trim($text);
  // $trimmed will be "Trim this"
  ```

- **str_replace($search, $replace, $string)**: Replaces all occurrences of a substring with another substring.

  ```
  $text = "Hello, world!";
  $new_text = str_replace("world", "universe", $text);
  // $new_text will be "Hello, universe!"
  ```

- **strpos($string, $substring)** and **strrpos($string, $substring)**: Find the position of the first or last occurrence of a substring within a string. Returns false if not found.

```
$text = "Hello, world!";
$position = strpos($text, "world");
// $position will be 7
$last_position = strrpos($text, "o");
// $last_position will be 8
```

- **`substr($string, $start, $length)`**: Extracts a substring from a string.

```
$text = "Hello, world!";
$substring = substr($text, 7, 5);
// $substring will be "world"
```

- **`str_repeat($string, $count)`**: Repeats a string a specified number of times.

```
$text = "PHP ";
$repeated = str_repeat($text, 3);
// $repeated will be "PHP PHP PHP "
```

- **`implode ($glue, $pieces)`** and **`explode($delimiter, $string)`**: implode joins an array of strings into a single string using a specified glue, while explode splits a string into an array using a specified delimiter.

```
$array = ["apple", "banana", "orange"];
$imploded = implode(", ", $array);
// $imploded will be "apple, banana, orange" $exploded = explode(",
", $imploded);
 // $exploded will be ["apple", "banana", "orange"]
```

- **`sprintf($format, $arg1, $arg2, ...)`**: Produces a formatted string using placeholders.

```
$name = "Alice";
$age = 30;
$greeting = sprintf("My name is %s and I am %d years old.", $name,
$age);
// $greeting will be "My name is Alice and I am 30 years old."
```

Printing strings in PHP

In concluding this chapter on PHP strings and functions, we have embarked on a journey that has empowered you with essential skills for handling textual data in your web development.

In PHP, you can print strings to the standard output (usually the web browser or the console) using various methods. Here are the primary ways to print strings in PHP, as can be seen in *Figure 6.1*:

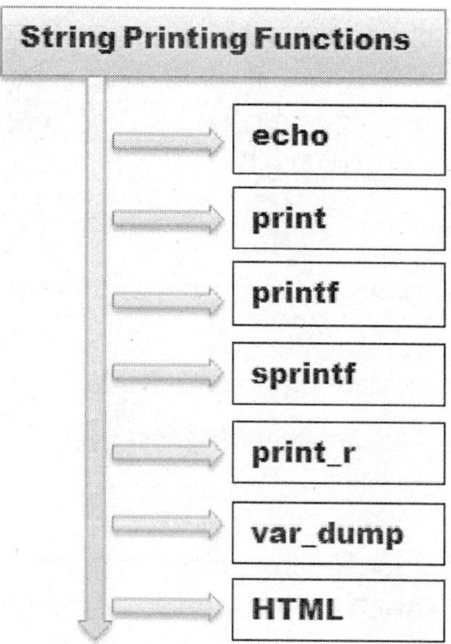

Figure 6.1: Ways to print strings in PHP

- Using **echo**:

  The **echo** statement is one of the most common ways to print strings in PHP. It can output one or more expressions separated by commas.

  echo does not return a value; it directly sends output to the browser or console.

  ```
  $message = "Hello, world!"; echo $message;
  ```

- Using **print**:

  The **print** statement is similar to echo, but it can only output a single expression.

  Like **echo**, **print** also does not return a value.

  ```
  $message = "Hello, world!"; print($message);
  ```

- Using **printf**:

  The **printf** function allows you to print formatted strings using placeholders.

  You provide a format string containing placeholders, followed by the values to substitute for those placeholders.

  ```
  $name = "Alice"; $age = 30; printf("Name: %s, Age: %d", $name, $age);
  ```

- Using **sprintf**:

  Similar to **printf**, the **sprintf** function formats a string but returns the formatted string instead of printing it directly.

This can be useful when you want to store the formatted string in a variable for later use.

```
$name = "Bob"; $age = 25; $formatted = sprintf("Name: %s, Age: %d", $name, $age); echo $formatted;
```

- Using **print_r**:

  The **print_r** function is used to print human-readable information about a variable, including its contents.

  It is commonly used for debugging and displaying arrays and objects.

  ```
  $myArray = [1, 2, 3]; print_r($myArray);
  ```

- Using **var_dump**:

  The **var_dump** function is similar to **print_r** but provides more detailed information about a variable, including data types and values.

  It is particularly useful for debugging and understanding variable structures.

  ```
  $myArray = [1, 2, 3]; var_dump($myArray);
  ```

- Using HTML:

  When working in a PHP script embedded in HTML, you can print strings directly within HTML tags using echo.

  ```
  <h1><?php echo "Welcome to my website!"; ?></h1>
  ```

These are the main ways to print strings in PHP. The choice of which method to use depends on your specific requirements, such as formatting, debugging, or integration with HTML.

Comparing strings

In PHP, you can compare strings using various comparison operators and functions. Here are some common methods for comparing strings in PHP:

- Equality comparison (== and ===)

  The == operator checks if two strings are equal in content. The === operator checks if two strings are not only equal in content but also have the same data type (string).

  ```
  $str1 = "Hello"; $str2 = "Hello";

   if ($str1 == $str2){

  echo "Equal";

  }
  ```

- Inequality comparison (!= and !==)

  The **!=** operator checks if two strings are not equal in content. The **!==** operator checks if two strings are either not equal in content or have different data types.

```
$str1 = "Hello";
$str2 = "World";
if ($str1 != $str2) {
echo "Not equal";
}
```

- String comparison functions:

  PHP provides several functions for comparing strings, such as **strcmp**, **strcasecmp**, **strnatcmp**, and **strnatcasecmp**. These functions return 0 if the strings are equal, a negative value if the first string is less than the second, and a positive value if the first string is greater than the second.

```
$str1 = "apple";
$str2 = "banana";
$result = strcmp($str1, $str2);
if ($result === 0) {
echo "Equal";
}
elseif ($result < 0) {
echo "str1 is less than str2";
}
else { echo "str1 is greater than str2";
}
```

- Case-insensitive comparison:

  To perform a case-insensitive comparison, you can use functions like **strcasecmp** or **strnatcasecmp**.

```
$str1 = "Hello";
$str2 = "hello";
if (strcasecmp($str1, $str2) === 0) {
echo "Case-insensitive equal";
}
```

- String length comparison:

  You can compare the lengths of two strings using **strlen** and then compare the lengths with the appropriate comparison operator.

```
$str1 = "apple";
$str2 = "banana";
if (strlen($str1) < strlen($str2)) {
echo "str1 is shorter than str2";
}
```

- Regular expression comparison:

  You can use regular expressions and functions like **preg_match** to compare strings based on more complex patterns.

```
$str = "Hello, World!";
if (preg_match("/^Hello/", $str)) {
echo "Starts with 'Hello'";
}
```

- **levenshtein()** function

  The **levenshtein()** function in PHP is used to calculate the Levenshtein distance between two strings. The Levenshtein distance, also known as the edit distance, is a measure of the similarity between two strings by counting the minimum number of single-character edits (insertions, deletions, or substitutions) required to transform one string into the other.

  Here is the basic syntax of the **levenshtein()** function:

```
int levenshtein(string $str1, string $str2, int $cost_insert = 1, int
$cost_delete = 1, int $cost_replace = 1): int
```

  - **$str1** and **$str2** are the two strings you want to compare.
  - **$cost_insert**, **$cost_delete**, and **$cost_replace** are optional parameters that allow you to assign custom costs to insertions, deletions, and substitutions. By default, each operation has a cost of 1.

The function returns an integer value, which is the Levenshtein distance between the two input strings. A smaller Levenshtein distance indicates a higher similarity between the strings, as it represents fewer required edits.

Here is an example of how to use the **levenshtein()** function:

```
$str1 = "kitten";
$str2 = "sitting";
```

```
$distance = levenshtein($str1, $str2);

echo "The Levenshtein distance between '$str1' and '$str2' is $distance.";
```

In this example, the Levenshtein distance between "kitten" and "sitting" is calculated, and the result is displayed. The function returns a distance of 3 because it takes three operations to transform "kitten" into "sitting" (substitute 'k' with 's,' insert 'i' after 't,' and insert 'g' at the end).

The **levenshtein()** function can be useful for tasks like spell checking, approximate string matching, and identifying similarities between strings in various applications.

- **soundex()** function:

  The **soundex()** function in PHP is used for phonetic text matching. It converts a given string into a four-character code that represents the way the string sounds when spoken. This code can be used for searching and comparing words that have similar pronunciations but may be spelled differently.

  Here is the basic syntax of the **soundex()** function:

  string soundex(string $string)

  $string is the input string for which you want to calculate the Soundex code.

  The **soundex()** function returns a string representing the Soundex code for the input string.

  Here is an example of how to use the **soundex()** function:

```
$word1 = "Smith";

$word2 = "Smyth";

$soundex1 = soundex($word1);

$soundex2 = soundex($word2);

if ($soundex1 === $soundex2) {

    echo "'$word1' and '$word2' have the same Soundex code: $soundex1";

} else {

echo "'$word1' and '$word2' have different Soundex codes: $soundex1 and $soundex2";

}
```

  In this example, the **soundex()** function is used to calculate the Soundex codes for the words "Smith" and "Smyth." The function returns the same Soundex code for both words because they have similar pronunciations.

  It is important to note that Soundex is a simple phonetic matching algorithm and may not always produce accurate results for all words, especially for names or words from different languages. More advanced phonetic matching algorithms like Metaphone or Double Metaphone are available for more accurate phonetic matching in PHP.

- **`metaphone()`** function:

  The **`metaphone()`** function in PHP is used for phonetic text matching, just like the **`soundex()`** function. However, **`metaphone()`** provides more accurate phonetic encoding than soundex and is capable of handling a wider range of language variations and word pronunciations. It produces a shorter code than soundex and is often used for tasks like spell-checking, approximate string matching, and searching for words with similar pronunciations.

  Here is the basic syntax of the **`metaphone()`** function:

  ```
  string metaphone(string $string, int $phonemes = 0)
  ```

  $string is the input string for which you want to calculate the Metaphone code.

  `$phonemes` is an optional parameter that specifies the maximum number of phonemes in the resulting code. If set to a positive integer, it limits the length of the Metaphone code. By default, it is set to 0, which means no length limit.

  The **`metaphone()`** function returns a string representing the Metaphone code for the input string.

  Here is an example of how to use the **`metaphone()`** function:

  ```
  $word1 = "knight";

  $word2 = "night";

  $metaphone1 = metaphone($word1);

  $metaphone2 = metaphone($word2);

  if ($metaphone1 === $metaphone2) {

      echo "'$word1' and '$word2' have the same Metaphone code: $metaphone1";

  } else {

      echo "'$word1' and '$word2' have different Metaphone codes: $metaphone1 and $metaphone2";

  }
  ```

In this example, the **`metaphone()`** function is used to calculate the Metaphone codes for the words "knight" and "night." The function returns the same Metaphone code for both words because they have similar pronunciations, even though they are spelled differently.

The **`metaphone()`** function is a more robust choice than **`soundex()`** for phonetic matching, as it can handle a wider variety of words and language variations.

So, the method you choose for comparing strings in PHP depends on your specific use case and the type of comparison you need (e.g., case-sensitive or case-insensitive). Use the appropriate operator or function accordingly to achieve the desired comparison results.

Conclusion

In concluding this chapter on PHP strings and functions, we've embarked on a journey that has empowered you with essential skills for handling textual data in your web development projects. You have learned how to declare and manipulate strings, combining them to create dynamic content, and even how to interpolate variables seamlessly. Moreover, we've delved into the extensive toolbox of PHP's string functions, providing you with a versatile set of tools to tackle a wide range of text-related tasks.

As you continue your PHP development journey, remember that strings are not mere characters; they are the lifeblood of user interaction and content presentation. Mastery of PHP strings and functions opens doors to crafting engaging and interactive web applications. Whether you're building web forms, processing user input, generating dynamic HTML, or working with databases, the knowledge gained in this chapter will serve as a valuable foundation. Keep exploring, experimenting, and applying what you've learned, and you will find that your ability to create compelling web experiences will continue to grow. The world of web development is at your fingertips, and PHP strings are your versatile tools to shape it.

Points to remember

- **Strings**: PHP strings are sequences of characters enclosed in single or double quotes.
- **Concatenation**: Use the . operator to concatenate strings.
- **String length**: Determine the length of a string with strlen().
- **String interpolation**: In double-quoted strings, you can embed variables with curly braces.
- **Escape characters**: Use \ to escape special characters within strings.
- **String functions**: PHP provides various functions for string manipulation, like substr(), str_replace(), strpos(), and more.
- **Case sensitivity**: PHP is case-sensitive for string comparisons.
- **String conversion**: Convert between data types and strings using functions like strval() and intval().
- **Escape sequences**: Use escape sequences like \n and \t for special characters.

- **String comparison**: Use == or === for string comparisons.
- **String splitting**: Split strings into arrays with functions like explode().
- **String formatting**: Use sprintf() for string formatting with placeholders.
- **Character encoding**: Be aware of character encoding, especially for international text, and consider using mb_strlen() and mb_substr() for multibyte encodings.

CHAPTER 7
PHP File Handling

Introduction

File handling is a fundamental aspect of programming, and PHP offers a robust set of functions and methods for working with files. In this chapter, we will explore the world of file handling in PHP. From reading and writing files to managing directories and handling file uploads, PHP provides a versatile toolkit to interact with files on the server. We will delve into the various file functions available in PHP, covering everything from basic operations to advanced techniques. Whether you need to create, read, modify, or delete files, this chapter will equip you with the knowledge and skills to handle files effectively within your PHP applications. Let us dive in and discover the power of file handling in PHP.

Structure

The chapter covers the following topics:

- File handling in PHP
- File functions

Objectives

The primary objective of this chapter is to provide a comprehensive understanding of file handling in PHP, with a focus on exploring the essential file functions and techniques.

File handling in PHP

PHP provides a set of functions and methods for handling files, which includes creating, reading, writing, and manipulating files on the server's file system. Here is an overview of some common file-handling operations in PHP:

- **For opening and closing files**
  - `fopen()`: Opens a file or URL for reading or writing and returns a file pointers resource. It requires two parameters: the file name or path and the mode.

    The syntax of `fopen()` is as follows:

    ```
    resource fopen ( string $filename , string $mode [, bool $use_include_path = false [, resource $context ]] )
    ```

    In this syntax:

    - `$filename` is the name of the file or URL to open
    - `$mode` is the mode in which to open the file. This can be one of the following:
    - '`r`': read-only
    - '`w`': write only (truncates the file to zero length or creates a new file)
    - '`a`': append-only (opens the file for writing at the end of the file)
    - '`x`': exclusive write (creates a new file and opens it for writing only if it does not already exist)
    - '`b`': binary mode (used in conjunction with the above modes to indicate that the file should be opened in binary mode)
    - '`t`': text mode (used in conjunction with the above modes to indicate that the file should be opened in text mode)
    - `$use_include_path` is a boolean parameter that indicates whether to search for the file in the include path (if set)
    - `$context` is an optional parameter that allows you to specify a context for the file stream (for example, HTTP headers, SSL settings, etc.)

Here is an example that demonstrates how to use `fopen()` to open a file in read-only mode, read its contents line by line, and then close the file:

```
$file = fopen('data.txt', 'r');

   if ($file) {
       while (($line = fgets($file)) !== false) {
           echo $line;
```

```
    }
    fclose($file);
}
```

In this example, the file data.txt is opened in read-only mode using **`fopen()`**. The while loop reads the file line by line using the **`fgets()`** function, and the contents of each line are echoed to the screen. Finally, the **`fclose()`** function is called to close the file.

- **`fclose()`:**

  The PHP **`fclose()`** function is used to close an open file pointer or handle in PHP. It is typically used after a file has been opened using **`fopen()`** or a related function.

  Here is the syntax for the **`fclose()`** function:

  ```
  bool fclose ( resource $handle )
  ```

  The function takes a single parameter, which is the file pointer or handles to be closed. The function returns a boolean value indicating whether the file was successfully closed or not.

Example:

```
<?php
// Open a file for writing
$file = fopen("example.txt", "w");

// Write some data to the file
fwrite($file, "Hello, world!");

// Close the file
fclose($file);
?>
```

- **For reading files:**

  After opening a file, you can read its contents using functions like **`fgets()`** or **`fread()`**. The PHP **`fread()` function is used to read a specified number of bytes from a file. It is a file-handling function in PHP that allows you to read data from a file.**

  Syntax:

  ```
  fread($file_handle, $length)
  ```

`$file_handle`: Required. Specifies the file pointer or file handle to read from.

`$length`: Required. Specifies the number of bytes to read from the file.

Return value:

Returns the read data as a string.

- `fgets()`: Reads a line from an open file.
- `file_get_contents()`: Reads the entire contents of a file into a string.

Example:

```
$file = fopen("example.txt", "r");
$line = fgets($file);
$content = fread($file, 1024);
$contents = file_get_contents("example.txt");
fclose($file);
```

- **For writing to files:**

  To write to a file, you can use functions like `fwrite()` or `file_put_contents()`.

  The PHP `fwrite()` **function is used to write data to a file. It takes three parameters: a file pointer, a string to be written, and an optional parameter that specifies the maximum number of bytes to write.**

  Here is the syntax of the `fwrite()` function:

```
fwrite ( resource $handle , string $string [, int $length ] ) :
int|false
```

  - **resource $handle**: A file pointer, which is a reference to the opened file. It can be obtained using functions such as `fopen()`, `fsockopen()`, and `tmpfile()`.
  - **string $string**: The string to be written to the file.
  - **int $length**: An optional parameter that specifies the maximum number of bytes to be written. If this parameter is not specified, all the data in the string will be written to the file.

The `fwrite()` function returns the number of bytes written to the file or false on error.

Here is an example of how to use the `fwrite()` function to write data to a file:

`fwrite()`: Writes a string to an open file.

```
$file = fopen("example.txt", "w"); // Open for writing
fwrite($file, "Hello, World!");
fclose($file);
```

In this example, we first open a file named "example.txt" in write mode using the **fopen()** function. Then we write the string "Hello, World!\n" to the file using the **fwrite()** function.

Alternatively, you can use **file_put_contents()** to write data to a file in a single line.

- **For checking file existence**
    - **file_exists()**: Checks if a file or directory exists.
    - **is_file()**: Checks if a given path is a regular file.

```
if (file_exists("example.txt")) {
echo "File exists.";
}
if (is_file("example.txt")) {
echo "It's a regular file.";
}
```

- **For file information**
    - **filesize()**: Returns the file size in bytes.
    - **filetype()**: Returns the file type (e.g., file, directory).
    - **filectime(), filemtime(), fileatime()**: Return file creation, modification, and access times.

```
$size = filesize("example.txt");
$type = filetype("example.txt");
$created = filectime("example.txt");
$modified = filemtime("example.txt");
```

- **For deleting files**

  In PHP, the **unlink()** function is used to delete a file from the file system. It accepts a single argument, which is the path to the file that needs to be deleted.

  unlink(): Deletes a file.

```
if (file_exists("example.txt")) {
unlink("example.txt");
}
```

- **For directory operations**
    - **mkdir()**: Creates a new directory.

- **`rmdir()`**: Removes a directory.
- **`scandir()`**: Lists files and directories in a directory.

```
mkdir("new_directory");
rmdir("old_directory");
$files = scandir("directory_path");
```

- **File uploads (HTML forms)**

  PHP provides features to handle file uploads in web applications. When a file is uploaded through a form, it is stored in a temporary location. When handling file uploads from HTML forms, you can use the **`$_FILES`** superglobal to access the uploaded file's information.

```
$uploadedFile = $_FILES['file_input_name'];
$fileName = $uploadedFile['name'];
$fileTmpName = $uploadedFile['tmp_name'];
$fileSize = $uploadedFile['size'];
$fileType = $uploadedFile['type'];
move_uploaded_file($fileTmpName, "uploads/" . $fileName);
```

Remember to handle file uploads with care and ensure proper security measures to prevent malicious uploads.

These are some of the basic file-handling operations in PHP. When working with files, it is crucial to handle errors gracefully, check file permissions, and sanitize user inputs to maintain the security and integrity of your applications.

File functions

In addition to the file handling functions and methods mentioned earlier, PHP provides a variety of other file-related functions that offer different functionalities and capabilities. Here are some additional PHP file functions:

- **File copy and move**
  - **`copy()`**: Copies a file.
  - **`rename()`**: Renames a file or directory.

```
copy("source.txt", "destination.txt");
rename("old_name.txt", "new_name.txt");
```

- **File permissions**
  - **`chmod()`**: Changes file permissions.

- **`chown()`**: Changes file owner.
- **`chgrp()`**: Changes file group.

```
chmod("file.txt", 0644); // Change file permissions to read-write for owner, read-only    for others
chown("file.txt", "new_owner");
chgrp("file.txt", "new_group");
```

- **File locking**
  - **`flock()`**: Locks or unlocks a file.

    ```
    $file = fopen("example.txt", "w");
    if (flock($file, LOCK_EX)) {
    // Exclusive lock acquired, perform operations
    flock($file, LOCK_UN); // Release the lock
    }
    fclose($file);
    ```

- **File information**
  - **`stat()`**: Returns file information as an array.
  - **`pathinfo()`**: Returns information about a file path.
  - **`realpath()`**: Returns the absolute path of a file.

    ```
    $fileInfo = stat("example.txt");
    $pathInfo = pathinfo("example.txt");
    $realPath = realpath("example.txt");
    ```

- **Temporary files**
  - **`tempnam()`**: Generates a unique temporary file name.
  - **`tmpfile()`**: Creates a temporary file.

    ```
    $tempFile = tempnam("/tmp", "prefix");
    $tempHandle = tmpfile();
    ```

- **File iteration**
  - **`file()`**: Reads an entire file into an array, with each line as an element.
  - **`fpassthru()`**: Output all remaining data from a file pointer.
  - **`fgetcsv()`**: Reads a line from a CSV file.

    ```
    $lines = file("example.txt");
    ```

```
$csvFile = fopen("data.csv", "r");
while (($data = fgetcsv($csvFile)) !== false) {
// Process CSV data
}
fclose($csvFile);
```

- **File compression**
  - **`gzopen()`, `gzwrite()`, `gzread()`:** Functions for working with compressed (gzip) files.
  - **`zip_open()`, `zip_read()`:** Functions for working with ZIP archives.

```
$gzipFile = gzopen("compressed.gz", "rb");
while (!feof($gzipFile)) {
  $data = gzread($gzipFile, 4096);
 // Process compressed data
}
gzclose($gzipFile);
```

These are some additional PHP file functions that provide various capabilities for working with files, directories, and file-related operations. Depending on your specific requirements, you can choose the appropriate function to accomplish your file-handling tasks.

Conclusion

In conclusion, this chapter has equipped you with a solid foundation in file handling within PHP. You have learned about various file functions and techniques, enabling you to create, read, write, and manipulate files and directories effectively. Armed with this knowledge, you are now better prepared to develop PHP applications that can seamlessly interact with files, making your coding journey more versatile and efficient.

Points to remember

- **Opening and closing files:** Use **`fopen()`** to open files for reading or writing and **fclose()** to close them when done.
- **Reading files:** Functions like **`fgets()`**, **`fread()`**, and **`file_get_contents()`** enable reading file content.
- **Writing to files:** Use **`fwrite()`** to write data to files opened for writing.

- **Checking file existence:** Functions like **`file_exists()`** and **`is_file()`** help check if files exist and are regular files.
- **File information:** **`filesize()`**, **`filetype()`**, **`filectime()`**, **`filemtime()`**, and **`fileatime()`** provide file information.
- **Deleting files:** **`unlink()`** is used to delete files.
- **Directory operations:** **`mkdir()`** and **`rmdir()`** create and remove directories, while **`scandir()`** lists directory contents.
- **File locking:** **`flock()`** allows for file locking to prevent concurrent access issues.
- **File permissions:** Use **`chmod()`**, **`chown()`**, and **`chgrp()`** to manage file permissions and ownership.
- **Temporary files:** **`tempnam()`** generates unique temporary file names, and **`tmpfile()`** creates temporary files.
- **File iteration:** Functions like **`file()`**, **`fpassthru()`**, and **`fgetcsv()`** facilitate file content iteration.
- **File compression:** PHP offers functions for working with compressed files, such as **`gzopen()`**, **`gzwrite()`**, and **`zip_open()`**.

CHAPTER 8
PHP Database Operations

Introduction

PHP database integration is a crucial aspect of web development that allows websites and applications to interact with and manage data stored in databases. PHP, a versatile server-side scripting language, provides the tools and functions to establish connections to various database management systems such as MySQL, PostgreSQL, and SQLite. This integration enables developers to perform essential database operations like data retrieval, insertion, modification, and deletion seamlessly within their web applications. By harnessing the power of PHP's database integration capabilities, developers can create dynamic and data-driven websites that respond to user input and deliver personalized content, making the user experience more interactive and engaging.

Structure

The chapter covers the following topics:

- Introduction to databases
- Database operations
- Creating table in PHP
- Connecting to MYSQL database
- Database handling functions

Objectives

The objective of this chapter is to provide readers with a comprehensive understanding of databases and their role in software development. We begin by introducing the concept of databases and their significance in storing, managing, and retrieving structured data. Subsequently, we explore various database operations, emphasizing the importance of data manipulation, retrieval, and maintenance. The chapter then delves into practical aspects, guiding readers on how to create database tables using PHP and establish connections to MySQL databases. Additionally, it equips readers with essential knowledge about database handling functions, empowering them to interact with and manage data effectively. Ultimately, the goal is to equip readers with a solid foundation in database concepts and practical skills that are essential for developing data-driven applications.

Introduction to databases

Databases play a pivotal role in web development, and in the context of PHP, they serve as the backbone for storing and managing data. PHP, a server-side scripting language, seamlessly integrates with various database management systems like MySQL, PostgreSQL, SQLite, and others. These databases are where you store critical information, such as user profiles, product catalogs, and content. PHP facilitates database interactions by providing functions and extensions that allow you to establish connections, execute queries, and process results. This integration empowers web developers to build dynamic and data-driven applications, ranging from e-commerce websites with real-time product updates to content management systems that organize and deliver content efficiently. Understanding databases in the PHP context is fundamental for creating robust, interactive, and personalized web experiences that cater to the needs of users and businesses alike.

Database integration with PHP applications

Creating a database in PHP typically involves interacting with a **Database Management System** (**DBMS**) like MySQL, PostgreSQL, SQLite, or others. Here is a step-by-step guide on how to create a database using PHP and MySQL as an example:

1. **Install and set up the database server:** Ensure that you have a MySQL server installed and running on your web server. You will need to know the server's host, username, and password to connect to it. You can also use phpMyAdmin or a similar tool to manage your databases if you prefer a graphical interface.

2. **Install the PHP MySQL extension (if not already installed):** If you are not sure whether the PHP MySQL extension is installed, you can check by creating a PHP script with the following content and accessing it through a web browser:

```
<?
php phpinfo();
        ?>
```

Look for the MySQL section in the **phpinfo()** output. If it is not installed, you may need to install it. In modern PHP versions, you can use PDO or mysqli as alternatives.

3. **Create a PHP Script to create a database:** Here is a simple example of a PHP script that creates a MySQL database:

```
<?php
// Database connection parameters
$host = 'localhost';  // Replace with your MySQL server host
$username = 'root';  // Replace with your MySQL username
$password = 'password';  // Replace with your MySQL password

// Create a connection to MySQL
$conn = new mysqli($host, $username, $password);

// Check connection
if ($conn->connect_error) {
    die("Connection failed: " . $conn->connect_error);
}

// Create a new database
$sql = "CREATE DATABASE mydatabase";
if ($conn->query($sql) === TRUE) {
    echo "Database created successfully";
} else {
    echo "Error creating database: " . $conn->error;
}

// Close the MySQL connection
$conn->close();
?>
```

Replace **$host**, **$username**, and **$password** with your MySQL server's details. This script connects to MySQL, creates a new database named "mydatabase," and then closes the connection.

4. **Access the script in your web browser:** Save the script with a **.php** extension (for example, **create_database.php**) and upload it to your web server. Access the script through your web browser (for example, **http://yourdomain.com/**

create_database.php). If everything is set up correctly, you should see a message indicating that the database was created successfully.

To secure your PHP scripts that interact with the database, especially when handling user input, to prevent SQL injection and other security vulnerabilities. It is also a good practice to put your database connection details in a separate configuration file and use include or require to include it in your PHP scripts for better code organization and security.

Creating table in PHP

In PHP, you can create tables in various ways depending on your use case. One common way is to create an HTML table dynamically using PHP code to fetch data from a database or generate table rows based on some logic. Here is a basic example of how to create an HTML table in PHP:

```
<!DOCTYPE html>
<html>
<head>
    <title>PHP Table Example</title>
</head>
<body>
    <table border="1">
        <thead>
            <tr>
                <th>ID</th>
                <th>Name</th>
                <th>Email</th>
            </tr>
        </thead>
        <tbody>
            <?php
            // Sample data (you can replace this with data from a database)
            $data = [
             ['id' => 1, 'name' => 'John Doe', 'email' => 'john@example.com'],
             ['id' => 2, 'name' => 'Jane Smith', 'email' => 'jane@example.com'],
             ['id' => 3, 'name' => 'Bob Johnson', 'email' => 'bob@example.com'],
            ];

            // Loop through the data and generate table rows
```

```
        foreach ($data as $row) {
            echo '<tr>';
            echo '<td>' . $row['id'] . '</td>';
            echo '<td>' . $row['name'] . '</td>';
            echo '<td>' . $row['email'] . '</td>';
            echo '</tr>';
        }
        ?>
    </tbody>
  </table>
</body>
</html>
```

In this example:

We start an HTML document and create a table using the **<table>, <thead>, <tbody>**, and **<tr>** elements. In the table, we define the table headers using **<th>** elements. We define sample data in a PHP array (**$data**) to simulate data retrieval from a database. We use a foreach loop to iterate through the data and generate table rows (**<tr>**) dynamically. Inside the loop, we use echo to output the table cells (**<td>**) with data from the array.

You can replace the sample data in the $data array with data from your database or any other data source. This is a basic example, and you can customize it further based on your specific requirements.

Connecting to MYSQL database

To connect to a MySQL database server from PHP, you can use the mysqli extension or the **PHP Data Objects (PDO)** extension. You can find examples for both methods here:

- Using the mysqli extension:

```
<?php
// Database credentials
$hostname = "localhost"; // Replace with your MySQL server hostname
or IP address
$username = "your_username"; // Replace with your MySQL username
$password = "your_password"; // Replace with your MySQL password
$database = "your_database"; // Replace with the name of your MySQL
database

// Create a connection to the MySQL database
```

```
$mysqli = new mysqli($hostname, $username, $password, $database);

// Check if the connection was successful
if ($mysqli->connect_error) {
    die("Connection failed: " . $mysqli->connect_error);
}

// Now you can perform database operations using $mysqli

// Example: Query the database
$query = "SELECT * FROM your_table";
$result = $mysqli->query($query);

if ($result) {
    while ($row = $result->fetch_assoc()) {
        echo "ID: " . $row["id"] . " - Name: " . $row["name"] .
"<br>";
    }
    $result->free(); // Free the result set
} else {
    echo "Error: " . $mysqli->error;
}

// Close the database connection
$mysqli->close();
?>
```

- Using PDO:

```
<?php
// Database credentials
$hostname = "localhost"; // Replace with your MySQL server hostname
or IP address
$username = "your_username"; // Replace with your MySQL username
$password = "your_password"; // Replace with your MySQL password
$database = "your_database"; // Replace with the name of your MySQL
database
```

```
try {
    // Create a PDO database connection
    $pdo = new PDO("mysql:host=$hostname;dbname=$database",
$username, $password);

    // Set PDO to throw exceptions on errors
    $pdo->setAttribute(PDO::ATTR_ERRMODE, PDO::ERRMODE_EXCEPTION);

    // Now you can perform database operations using $pdo

    // Example: Query the database
    $query = "SELECT * FROM your_table";
    $stmt = $pdo->query($query);

    while ($row = $stmt->fetch()) {
        echo "ID: " . $row["id"] . " - Name: " . $row["name"] .
"<br>";
    }
} catch (PDOException $e) {
    die("Error: " . $e->getMessage());
}

// Close the database connection (not necessary with PDO, as it's
automatically closed)
$pdo = null;
?>
```

These examples establish a connection to your MySQL database and demonstrate a basic query.

Database handling functions

PHP provides a variety of functions and libraries for working with databases, particularly MySQL. Here are some commonly used functions and libraries for database handling in PHP:

- **MySQL Improved Extension (MySQLi):** MySQLi is an improved version of the older MySQL extension in PHP. It provides both an object-oriented and procedural API for interacting with MySQL databases. In PHP, the MySQLi extension offers a set of functions to interact with MySQL databases. These functions empower developers to establish connections, execute queries, fetch results, implement prepared statements for enhanced security, and close database connections. Below are essential MySQLi functions that play important roles in database operations:

- **`mysqli_connect()`:** Establishes a connection to a MySQL database server.
- **`mysqli_query()`:** Executes a MySQL query.
- **`mysqli_fetch_assoc()`:** Fetches a result row as an associative array.
- **`mysqli_prepare() and mysqli_stmt_bind_param()`:** Used for prepared statements to prevent SQL injection.
- **`mysqli_close()`:** Closes a previously opened database connection.

Example:

```
$conn = mysqli_connect("localhost", "username", "password",
"database");

$result = mysqli_query($conn, "SELECT * FROM table");

while ($row = mysqli_fetch_assoc($result)) {

    echo $row['column_name'];

}

mysqli_close($conn);
```

- **PDO:** PDO is a database abstraction layer in PHP that supports multiple database management systems. It offers a consistent API for working with databases. In PHP, the **PHP Data Objects** (**PDO**) extension provides a powerful and flexible interface for database connectivity. Below are key functions commonly used in conjunction with PDO to interact with databases, perform SQL queries, and manage transactions:
  - **`new PDO()`:** Creates a new PDO instance for database connections.
  - **`prepare()`:** Prepares an SQL statement for execution.
  - **`execute()`:** Executes a prepared statement.
  - **`fetch()`:** Fetches the next row from a result set.
  - **`beginTransaction(), commit(), and rollback()`:** Used for database transactions.

Example:

```
$pdo = new PDO("mysql:host=localhost;dbname=database", "username",
"password");
```

```
$stmt = $pdo->prepare("SELECT * FROM table");
$stmt->execute();
while ($row = $stmt->fetch(PDO::FETCH_ASSOC)) {
    echo $row['column_name'];
}
$pdo = null; // Close the connection
```

- **MySQL Functions (deprecated):** The original MySQL extension is deprecated as of PHP 5.5 and removed in PHP 7. Instead, you should use MySQLi or PDO for database operations.
- **Database abstraction libraries:** There are also several third-party database abstraction libraries and frameworks available for PHP, such as Doctrine and Laravel's Eloquent, which provide higher-level abstractions for database interactions.

To handle database connections securely, use prepared statements or parameterized queries to prevent SQL injection, and properly sanitize user input when working with databases in PHP.

Following is the PHP program that creates a table and inserts a record into it using MySQL as the database:

```
<?php
// Database connection parameters
$host = 'localhost';      // Replace with your MySQL server host
$username = 'root';       // Replace with your MySQL username
$password = 'password';  // Replace with your MySQL password
$database = 'mydatabase'; // Replace with your database name

// Create a connection to MySQL
$conn = new mysqli($host, $username, $password, $database);

// Check connection
if ($conn->connect_error) {
    die("Connection failed: " . $conn->connect_error);
}

// SQL query to create a table
```

```
$sqlCreateTable = "CREATE TABLE IF NOT EXISTS users (
    id INT AUTO_INCREMENT PRIMARY KEY,
    first_name VARCHAR(50) NOT NULL,
    last_name VARCHAR(50) NOT NULL,
    email VARCHAR(100) NOT NULL
)";

if ($conn->query($sqlCreateTable) === TRUE) {
    echo "Table 'users' created successfully.<br>";

    // SQL query to insert a record into the table
    $sqlInsertRecord = "INSERT INTO users (first_name, last_name, email)
    VALUES ('John', 'Doe', 'john@example.com')";

    if ($conn->query($sqlInsertRecord) === TRUE) {
        echo "Record inserted successfully.";
    } else {
        echo "Error inserting record: " . $conn->error;
    }
} else {
    echo "Error creating table: " . $conn->error;
}

// Close the MySQL connection
$conn->close();
?>
```

The above code connects to the MySQL database, checks if the "users" table exists, creates it if it does not, and then inserts a sample record into the table.

Conclusion

This chapter has provided a comprehensive introduction to databases and the fundamental operations involved in working with them. We explored the process of creating tables in PHP, emphasizing the importance of proper database design. Additionally, we learned how to establish connections to MySQL databases, a crucial step in any database-driven application. Lastly, we delved into essential database handling functions, which are essential tools for interacting with and managing data. This foundation of knowledge will serve as a valuable basis for building robust and efficient database-driven applications in PHP, empowering developers to create and manipulate data with confidence and precision.

In the upcoming chapter, we will dig into *Advanced PHP Concepts and Best Practices*, where we will explore techniques that uplift your coding proficiency, enhance application performance, and ensure the security and maintainability of your PHP projects. Let's board on a journey to deepen our understanding and improve our skills for developing high-quality PHP applications.

Points to remember

- **Understanding databases:** Gain a clear understanding of what databases are and their significance in organizing and storing structured data efficiently.
- **Database operations:** Get acquainted with essential database operations, such as inserting, updating, retrieving, and deleting data, as they are fundamental to working with databases.
- **Creating tables in PHP:** Learn how to create database tables using PHP code, ensuring that the table structure aligns with your data storage requirements.
- **Connecting to MySQL database:** Understand how to establish a connection between your PHP application and a MySQL database, including providing the necessary credentials and handling connection errors.
- **Database handling functions:** Explore various PHP functions and methods for interacting with databases, including executing SQL queries, handling errors, and processing query results.
- **Database security:** Be aware of the importance of database security. Implement best practices such as prepared statements and input validation to protect against SQL injection and other security threats.
- **Data integrity:** Maintain data integrity by defining appropriate constraints and relationships within your database tables to ensure accurate and reliable data storage.
- **Efficiency and optimization:** Consider strategies for optimizing database operations, such as indexing, caching, and proper query design, to enhance application performance.

Join our book's Discord space

Join the book's Discord Workspace for Latest updates, Offers, Tech happenings around the world, New Release and Sessions with the Authors:

https://discord.bpbonline.com

Section - III

Advanced PHP Concepts and Best Practices

CHAPTER 9
Object-Oriented Programming in PHP

Introduction

Object-Oriented Programming (**OOP**) in PHP is a programming paradigm that emphasizes the organization of code into reusable and modular objects. In PHP, a class serves as a blueprint, defining the properties (attributes) and behaviors (methods) that objects created from that class will possess. OOP principles such as encapsulation, inheritance, and polymorphism allow developers to create clean, maintainable, and extensible code. Encapsulation ensures that the internal workings of an object are hidden from external access. At the same time, inheritance enables the creation of new classes that inherit the properties and methods of existing classes. Polymorphism allows different objects to respond to method calls in a class-specific manner, promoting flexibility and code reusability. PHP's robust support for OOP makes it a powerful language for building complex, organized, and efficient web applications.

Structure

The chapter covers the following topics:

- Object-oriented concepts supported by PHP
- Creating classes
- Creating objects

- Constructor and destructor
- Properties and methods
- Encapsulation
- Inheritance
- $this variable
- Overloading and overriding
- Abstract classes
- Polymorphism
- Interface
- Final keyword
- References

Objectives

The objective of this chapter is to provide a comprehensive understanding of Object-Oriented Programming concepts in PHP. It covers the creation and usage of classes and objects, defining properties and methods, and explores essential OOP principles such as encapsulation, access specifiers, and the 'this' variable. Additionally, the chapter delves into more advanced topics like constructors and destructors, method overloading and overriding, abstract classes, polymorphism, interfaces, and the use of the 'final' keyword. By the end of this chapter, readers should be well-equipped to design and implement robust, object-oriented PHP code, enabling them to create more organized and maintainable applications.

Object-oriented concepts supported by PHP

PHP is a versatile server-side scripting language that fully supports Object-Oriented Programming concepts. Here are the key OOP concepts supported by PHP:

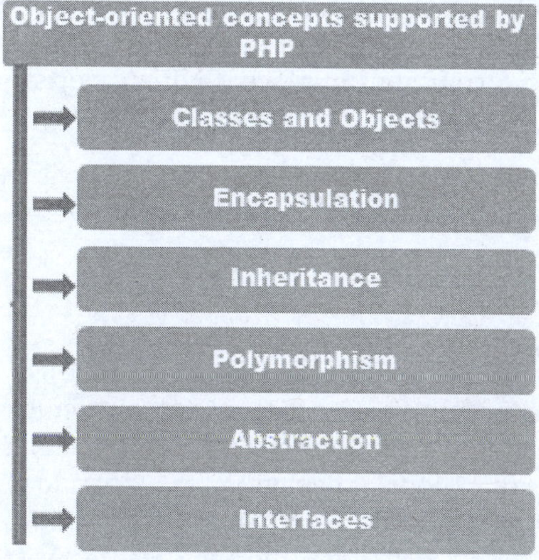

Figure 9.1: OOP concepts supported by PHP

Let us now talk about each concept in detail:

- **Classes and objects**: In PHP, a class is a blueprint or template for creating objects. It defines the structure and behavior of objects. Objects are instances of classes representing specific real-world entities or concepts. They encapsulate both data (attributes) and behavior (methods).
- **Encapsulation:** Encapsulation is the concept of bundling data (attributes or properties) and the methods (functions) that operate on that data into a single unit called a class. PHP supports access modifiers (public, private, and protected) to control the visibility and accessibility of class members.
- **Inheritance**: Inheritance allows you to create a new class (subclass or child class) based on an existing class (parent class or superclass). The child class inherits properties and methods from the parent class. PHP supports single inheritance, meaning a class can inherit from only one parent class. However, it supports multiple interfaces, allowing a class to implement multiple interfaces.
- **Polymorphism**: Polymorphism enables objects of different classes to respond to the same method or function call in a way that is specific to their class. In PHP, polymorphism is often achieved through method overriding, where a subclass provides its own implementation of a method defined in the parent class.
- **Abstraction**: Abstraction is the process of simplifying complex reality by modeling classes based on essential properties and behaviors while hiding unnecessary details. In PHP, you can create abstract classes and methods that must be implemented by concrete subclasses.

- **Interfaces:** An interface is a contract that defines a set of methods a class must implement. It allows for polymorphism by ensuring that objects of different classes adhere to a common interface. PHP supports interface declaration and implementation.

These OOP concepts in PHP help developers create well-structured, modular, and maintainable code. They are fundamental for building complex web applications, libraries, and frameworks.

Creating classes

A class in OOP is a draft or template that defines the structure and behavior of objects. It acts as a draft for creating instances of objects, encapsulating both data (attributes or properties) and methods (functions or behaviors) that operate on that data. Classes serve as a way to model and organize code around real-world entities or concepts. They allow you to create multiple objects that share the same characteristics and behaviors while maintaining a clear separation between different parts of your codebase. In essence, classes provide a blueprint for creating objects with consistent attributes and behaviors, promoting code reusability and maintainability.

Creating objects

An object in programming represents a specific instance of a class, following the draft or template defined by that class. Objects encapsulate both data (attributes or properties) and behaviors (methods or functions) that are associated with the class. They allow you to model and work with real-world entities or concepts in your code. Objects are self-contained, meaning they can maintain their own state (through attributes) and perform actions or operations (through methods). Object-oriented programming revolves around the concept of creating and interacting with objects to build modular, reusable, and organized code, making it easier to manage and maintain complex software systems.

Constructor and destructor

In PHP, constructors and destructors are special methods used in object-oriented programming to initialize and clean up objects when they are created and destroyed. Constructors are used for initialization, while destructors are used for cleanup tasks. Here is an explanation of each:

Constructor

A constructor is a special method in a PHP class that is automatically called when an instance of the class is created using the '**`new`**' keyword. The constructor method is typically named **`__construct()`**. It can take parameters to set initial values for object properties.

Constructors are used to perform any necessary setup or initialization tasks when an object is created. This can include initializing properties, establishing connections, or performing other setup operations.

Example of a constructor in PHP:

```
class MyClass {
    public $property;

    public function __construct($initialValue) {
        $this->property = $initialValue;
        echo "Object created with value: $initialValue";
    }
}
$obj = new MyClass("Hello, world!");
```

Destructor

A destructor is another special method in PHP, named **`__destruct()`**. It is automatically called when an object is destroyed or goes out of scope (for example, when the script execution ends or when the **`unset()`** function is used).

Destructors are primarily used for performing cleanup tasks, such as closing database connections, releasing resources, or finalizing operations that need to occur before an object is destroyed.

Example of a destructor in PHP:

```
class MyClass {
    public function __construct() {
        echo "Object created";
    }
public function __destruct() {
        echo "Object destroyed";
    }
}
$obj = new MyClass();
// The destructor will be automatically called when the script ends, or
when you unset() $obj.
```

It is important to note that while constructors are automatically called when an object is created, destructors are automatically called when an object is destroyed, but you do not explicitly call them. They are mainly used for cleanup operations and are not required in most cases.

In PHP, you can have only one constructor and one destructor in a class, and they are automatically called when the corresponding events occur. Constructors help set up an object's initial state, while destructors help clean up resources or perform final actions before an object is destroyed.

Properties and methods

Properties and methods are fundamental concepts in OOP that are used to define the structure and behavior of objects within a class. Here is an explanation of properties and methods:

Properties (attributes)

Properties, also known as attributes or fields, are variables that hold data associated with an object. They define the characteristics or state of an object.

Properties are used to represent and store information about the object. For example, in a **`Person`** class, **`name`** and **`age`** could be properties to store the person's name and age. They are defined within the class and are often declared with access modifiers (for example, **public**, **private**, **protected**) to control their visibility and accessibility from outside the class.

Methods (functions)

Methods, also known as functions or behaviors, are functions defined within a class that perform actions or operations related to the object's behavior. Methods allow you to define what an object can do or how it can interact with its data. For example, a Person class might have a **`greet()`** method to allow the person to say hello.

Methods can access and modify the object's properties and are responsible for encapsulating the logic associated with the object's behavior. Like properties, methods can also have access modifiers to control their visibility and accessibility.

An example of creating a simple class in PHP

```
<?php
// Define a class called 'Person'
class Person {
    // Properties (attributes)
    public $name;
    public $age;
```

```
    // Constructor method
    public function __construct($name, $age) {
        $this->name = $name;
        $this->age = $age;
    }

    // Method to introduce the person
    public function introduce() {
        echo "Hello, my name is {$this->name}, and I am {$this->age} years
old.\n";
    }
}

// Create an instance (object) of the 'Person' class
$person1 = new Person("Alice", 30);

// Access and modify object properties
$person1->name = "Alice Smith";

// Call the 'introduce' method
$person1->introduce();

// Create another instance
$person2 = new Person("Bob", 25);
$person2->introduce();
?>
```

In this example:

1. We define a class called **Person** with properties (attributes) **$name** and **$age**.
2. The constructor method **__construct** is used to initialize these properties when a **Person** object is created.
3. We also define a method **introduce** within the class to display information about the person.
4. We create two instances of the **Person** class (**$person1** and **$person2**) and set their properties.

5. We call the **introduce** method for each person to introduce them.

This demonstrates the basic structure and usage of a PHP class to create and work with objects.

Encapsulation

Encapsulation is one of the fundamental principles of OOP that is used to restrict direct access to an object's properties and methods, while providing a controlled interface to interact with the object. In PHP, you can achieve encapsulation using access specifiers (public, protected, and private) and getter and setter methods. Here is how encapsulation works in PHP:

Access specifier

In OOP, access specifiers are used to control the visibility and accessibility of class properties and methods. PHP supports three primary access specifiers: public, protected, and private. Here is an explanation of each:

- **Public**: When a property or method is declared as public, it can be accessed from outside the class, both from within the class itself and from instances of the class.

```
class MyClass {
    public $publicVar;

    public function publicMethod() {
        echo "This is a public method.";
    }
}

$obj = new MyClass();
echo $obj->publicVar; // Accessing a public property
$obj->publicMethod(); // Calling a public method
```

- **Protected:** When a property or method is declared as protected, it can only be accessed from within the class itself and its subclasses (inheritance).

```
class MyClass {
    protected $protectedVar;

    protected function protectedMethod() {
```

```
        echo "This is a protected method.";
    }
}

class SubClass extends MyClass {
    public function accessProtected() {
        echo $this->protectedVar; // Accessing a protected property
        $this->protectedMethod(); // Calling a protected method
    }
}

$obj = new SubClass();
$obj->accessProtected(); // This will work
echo $obj->protectedVar; // This will result in an error
```

- **Private:** When a property or method is declared as private, it can only be accessed from within the class itself. It is not accessible from subclasses or outside the class.

```
class MyClass {
    private $privateVar;

    private function privateMethod() {
        echo "This is a private method.";
    }
}

class SubClass extends MyClass {
    // You cannot access private properties or methods in the subclass
}

$obj = new MyClass();
echo $obj->privateVar; // This will result in an error
$obj->privateMethod(); // This will result in an error
```

Example of encapsulation using access specifiers:

```
class MyClass {
    public $publicVar;
    protected $protectedVar;
    private $privateVar;
}
$obj = new MyClass();
$obj->publicVar = "This is public data";
// $obj->protectedVar and $obj->privateVar cannot be accessed from outside
the class
```

Access specifiers help enforce encapsulation, which is a fundamental OOP concept. They control how data and functionality are exposed and accessed in a class, promoting better code organization and maintenance. Developers use these access specifiers to hide or restrict access to certain class members to prevent unintended modifications or misuse.

- **Getter and setter methods:** To access and modify private and protected properties, you can create getter and setter methods within the class. These methods provide controlled access to the properties.

Example of encapsulation using getter and setter methods:

```
class MyClass {
    private $privateVar;

    public function setPrivateVar($value) {
        $this->privateVar = $value;
    }

    public function getPrivateVar() {
        return $this->privateVar;
    }
}

$obj = new MyClass();
$obj->setPrivateVar("This is private data");
echo $obj->getPrivateVar(); // Accessing the private property using a
getter method
```

Encapsulation helps maintain the integrity and consistency of an object's data by hiding the internal details and providing controlled access. This ensures that external code cannot inadvertently or maliciously modify the object's properties and allows you to implement validation and business logic within getter and setter methods.

Encapsulation is a crucial concept in OOP because it promotes data hiding and allows for more modular, maintainable, and secure code.

Inheritance

In Object-Oriented Programming, inheritance is a fundamental concept that allows a class to inherit properties and behaviors from another class. In PHP, you can implement inheritance using the extends keyword. Let us go through the basics of inheritance in PHP:

Syntax:

```
class ParentClass {
    // properties and methods
}
class ChildClass extends ParentClass {
    // additional properties and methods
}
```

Example:

```
class Animal {
    public $name;

    public function __construct($name) {
        $this->name = $name;
    }

    public function speak() {
        echo "Animal speaks\n";
    }
}

class Dog extends Animal {
    public function bark() {
        echo "Woof!\n";
    }
}
```

```
// Creating an instance of the child class
$dog = new Dog("Buddy");

// Accessing properties and methods from the parent class
echo $dog->name;  // Output: Buddy
$dog->speak();    // Output: Animal speaks

// Accessing methods from the child class
$dog->bark();     // Output: Woof!
```

In this example, Dog is a subclass (or child class) of Animal, which is the superclass (or parent class). The extends keyword is used to establish this relationship. The Dog class inherits the properties and methods of the Animal class.

Constructor in Inheritance:

When a child class is instantiated, the constructor of the parent class is not automatically called. However, you can explicitly call the parent class constructor using the **`parent::__construct()`** method:

```
class Dog extends Animal {
    public function __construct($name, $breed) {
        parent::__construct($name);
        $this->breed = $breed;
    }
}
```

Overriding Methods:

If a method is defined in both the parent and child classes, the child class method will override the parent class method. This is known as method overriding.

```
class Dog extends Animal {
    public function speak() {
        echo "Dog barks\n";
    }
}

$dog = new Dog("Buddy");
$dog->speak();  // Output: Dog barks
```

Final Keyword:

You can use the final keyword to prevent a class from being inherited or a method from being overridden.

```
final class FinalClass {
    // Class members
}

class ChildClass extends FinalClass {
    // This will result in an error since FinalClass is marked as final.
}
class Animal {
    final public function speak() {
        // This method cannot be overridden in child classes.
    }
}
```

So, Inheritance is a powerful concept in OOP that allows code reuse and promotes a hierarchical structure. Child classes can extend and specialize the functionality of parent classes, providing a way to model relationships between different classes in your application.

$this variable

In PHP, **`$this`** is a special variable that is used within an object-oriented context. It refers to the current instance of the class and is used to access class properties and methods.

Here are some key points about **`$this`**:

- **Accessing class members**: You use **`$this`** to access properties and methods within the same class. This is particularly useful when you have class members with the same name as local variables or parameters.
- **Method calls**: **`$this`** is used to call other methods within the same class.

  ```
  class MyClass {
          public function method1() {
           // ...
          }
          public function method2() {
          // Call method1 using $this
          $this->method1();
          }
  }
  ```

- **Scope**: **`$this`** is only available within the context of an object created from a class. It does not have a meaning outside of the class context.
- **Static versus non-static**: **`$this`** is used in non-static methods (instance methods). In static methods, you do not have access to **`$this`** because static methods are associated with the class itself, not with instances of the class.

```
class MyClass {

        public static function staticMethod() {

                // You can't use $this in a static method

        }

}
```

So, **`$this`** is a reference to the current object instance in a PHP class and is used to access class properties and methods within that instance.

Overloading and overriding

In OOP with PHP, overloading and overriding are two important concepts related to class methods. Let us explore these concepts in PHP:

Method overloading

Method overloading refers to the ability to define multiple methods with the same name in a class but with different parameters or argument lists. PHP does not support method overloading in the traditional sense (as in some other languages like Java or C++). In PHP, only the last defined method with a given name will be effective, and previous definitions will be overwritten.

Here is an example that demonstrates how method overloading does not work in PHP:

```
class MyClass {
    public function myMethod($param1) {
        echo "Method with one parameter: $param1";
    }

    public function myMethod($param1, $param2) {
        echo "Method with two parameters: $param1, $param2";
    }
}
```

```
$obj = new MyClass();
$obj->myMethod('A'); // This will not work as expected; it will result in a
parse error.
```

As shown in the example, PHP does not support method overloading by method signature, and only the second method definition will be effective.

Method overriding

Method overriding is a mechanism where a subclass provides a specific implementation of a method that is already defined in its superclass (parent class). This allows a subclass to replace or extend the behavior of the inherited method.

To override a method in PHP, you use the **parent** keyword to call the superclass's implementation of the method. The subclass's method must have the same name, parameters, and access modifier as the method it is overriding.

Here is an example of method overriding in PHP:

```
class ParentClass {
    public function myMethod() {
        echo "Method in ParentClass";
    }
}

class ChildClass extends ParentClass {
    public function myMethod() {
        parent::myMethod(); // Call the parent class's method
        echo "Method in ChildClass";
    }
}

$obj = new ChildClass();
$obj->myMethod();
```

In this example, **ChildClass** overrides the **myMethod** from **ParentClass** and extends its behavior.

Method overriding is a key concept in inheritance, allowing child classes to provide their own implementations of methods from parent classes while preserving the method's signature and polymorphism. It is often used for customization and specialization of behavior in derived classes.

Abstract classes

Abstract classes are an important object-oriented programming concept in PHP. They serve as blueprints for other classes and are typically used as a foundation for creating more specialized classes. Abstract classes are not meant to be instantiated themselves but provide a common structure and interface for their derived classes. Here is how abstract classes work in PHP:

- **Defining an abstract class:**

  To define an abstract class in PHP, you use the **abstract** keyword. Abstract classes may contain both abstract methods (methods without an implementation) and concrete methods (methods with an implementation).

```
abstract class MyAbstractClass {
    abstract public function abstractMethod();

    public function concreteMethod() {
        echo "This is a concrete method.";
    }
}
```

- **Abstract methods:**

  Abstract methods are declared in an abstract class but do not have an implementation in the abstract class itself. Subclasses (classes that inherit from the abstract class) are required to provide an implementation for these abstract methods.

```
abstract class MyAbstractClass {
    abstract public function abstractMethod();
}
```

- **Concrete methods:** Concrete methods are fully implemented methods in an abstract class. These methods provide common functionality that can be shared by the derived classes.

```
abstract class MyAbstractClass {
    public function concreteMethod() {
        echo "This is a concrete method.";
    }
}
```

- **Creating subclasses:** Abstract classes are meant to be extended by other classes. To create a subclass that inherits from an abstract class, you use the extends keyword.

```
class MySubClass extends MyAbstractClass {
    public function abstractMethod() {
        echo "Implementation of abstractMethod in MySubClass.";
    }
}
```

- **Instantiating subclasses:** Subclasses can be instantiated, and they should provide implementations for all abstract methods declared in the parent abstract class.

```
$obj = new MySubClass();
$obj->abstractMethod(); // This will call the implementation in MySubClass
$obj->concreteMethod(); // This will call the concrete method in the abstract class
```

Abstract classes are used to establish a common interface or a set of methods that derived classes must implement. They promote code reusability and provide a level of structure and consistency in class hierarchies. Abstract classes are a crucial part of inheritance and polymorphism in object-oriented programming in PHP.

Polymorphism

Polymorphism is a fundamental object-oriented programming concept that allows objects of different classes to be treated as objects of a common superclass. It enables you to create more flexible and extensible code by allowing you to work with objects in a more generic way without needing to know their specific types. In PHP, polymorphism is achieved through method overriding and interfaces. Here is how polymorphism works in PHP:

Method overriding:

Polymorphism in PHP is primarily achieved through method overriding, which is the ability of a subclass to provide a specific implementation for a method that is already defined in its superclass (parent class).

Let us consider an example:

```
class Animal {
    public function makeSound() {
        echo "Animal makes a sound";
    }
}
class Dog extends Animal {
    public function makeSound() {
        echo "Dog barks";
```

```
    }
}
class Cat extends Animal {
    public function makeSound() {
        echo "Cat meows";
    }
}
```

In this example, Dog and Cat are subclasses of Animal. Each subclass overrides the **makeSound** method to provide its own implementation.

Using polymorphism:

Polymorphism allows you to work with objects of different types as if they were of the same type (the common parent class). This is typically achieved through method calls:

```
function animalSound(Animal $animal) {
    $animal->makeSound();
}
$dog = new Dog();
$cat = new Cat();
animalSound($dog); // Output: "Dog barks"
animalSound($cat); // Output: "Cat meows"
```

The **animalSound** function takes an object of the Animal class as an argument but can accept objects of any subclass of Animal. It demonstrates polymorphism in action.

Using interfaces:

Another way to achieve polymorphism in PHP is by using interfaces. An interface defines a contract that classes can implement, ensuring they provide specific methods. Different classes can implement the same interface, allowing them to be treated polymorphically.

```
interface Shape {
    public function calculateArea();
}
class Circle implements Shape {
    public function calculateArea() {
        // Implementation for calculating the area of a circle
    }
}
class Square implements Shape {
    public function calculateArea() {
        // Implementation for calculating the area of a square
```

```
    }
}
```

This allows you to work with different shape objects through a common interface:

```
function getArea(Shape $shape) {
    return $shape->calculateArea();
}
$circle = new Circle();
$square = new Square();
$circleArea = getArea($circle);
$squareArea = getArea($square);
```

Polymorphism simplifies code and allows for greater flexibility and extensibility in your object-oriented designs. It promotes reusability and can make your code more adaptable to changes and additions in the future.

Interface

An interface is a fundamental object-oriented programming concept that defines a contract for classes. Interfaces specify a set of methods that implementing classes must provide, but they do not contain any method implementations themselves. Interfaces are used to establish a common structure for classes that do not share a common ancestor (as in the case of inheritance), allowing objects of different classes to be treated polymorphically.

Here is how to define and use interfaces in PHP:

- **Defining an interface:**

  To declare an interface, you use the **`interface`** keyword. Inside the interface, you define method signatures without any implementation. For example:

  ```
  interface Shape {
      public function calculateArea();
      public function calculatePerimeter();
  }
  ```

  In this example, the **`Shape`** interface defines two methods that any class implementing it must provide: **`calculateArea`** and **`calculatePerimeter`**.

- **Implementing an interface:**

  To implement an interface in a class, you use the **`implements`** keyword. The implementing class must provide concrete implementations for all the methods declared in the interface.

```
class Circle implements Shape {
    private $radius;
    public function __construct($radius) {
        $this->radius = $radius;
    }
    public function calculateArea() {
        return pi() * pow($this->radius, 2);
    }
    public function calculatePerimeter() {
        return 2 * pi() * $this->radius;
    }
}
```

The **Circle** class implements the **Shape** interface by providing concrete implementations for both **calculateArea** and **calculatePerimeter**.

- **Using interfaces:**

  Once a class implements an interface, you can use the interface to work with objects of that class in a polymorphic way, treating them as instances of the interface.

```
function printShapeDetails(Shape $shape) {
    echo "Area: " . $shape->calculateArea() . "<br>";
    echo "Perimeter: " . $shape->calculatePerimeter() . "<br>";
}
$circle = new Circle(5);
printShapeDetails($circle);
```

In this example, the **printShapeDetails** function takes a **Shape** object as a parameter, and you can pass a **Circle** object to it because **Circle** implements the **Shape** interface.

Interfaces in PHP allow you to define a common structure that multiple classes can adhere to, ensuring that they provide specific methods. This promotes code consistency and polymorphism, making your code more flexible and adaptable to different scenarios and new classes.

Final keyword

In PHP, the **final** keyword is used to restrict the further modification or extension of classes, methods, and properties. When applied to a class, method, or property, the **final** keyword indicates that it cannot be subclassed (for classes), overridden (for methods), or redeclared (for properties). This helps enforce immutability and prevents accidental or intentional changes to specific parts of your code. Here is how the **final** keyword works in different contexts:

- **Final classes:** When a class is declared as **final**, it cannot be extended (subclassed). This means that you cannot create subclasses that inherit from the final class.

```
final class FinalClass {
    // Class implementation
}
You cannot create a subclass of FinalClass:

class SubClass extends FinalClass {
    // This will result in a compile-time error
}
```

- **Final methods:** When a method is declared as **final**, it cannot be overridden by subclasses. This ensures that the method's behavior remains consistent in all derived classes.

```
class ParentClass {
    final public function finalMethod() {
        // Method implementation
    }
}
class ChildClass extends ParentClass {
    // You cannot override finalMethod here
}
```

- **Final properties:** In PHP, properties (class variables) cannot be explicitly declared as **final**, like methods or classes. However, you can achieve a similar level of immutability by using getters and setters and by making the property **private** or **protected**.

```
class MyClass {
    protected $myProperty;

    final public function getMyProperty() {
        return $this->myProperty;
    }
}
```

By making the property **protected** and providing only a **final** getter method, you effectively prevent the property from being modified directly in subclasses.

The **final** keyword is used to ensure that specific aspects of your code remain unchanged, providing a level of predictability and stability. It is a valuable tool when you want to enforce immutability and maintain consistency in your class hierarchies. However, use it with caution, as it limits the flexibility of inheritance and overriding, which are powerful OOP concepts.

References

References are a way to create multiple variables that refer to the same underlying data. This concept is used to create aliases for variables, allowing multiple variables to point to the same value or object in memory. In object-oriented programming with PHP, references can be used to create multiple references to objects. Here is how references work with objects:

- **Creating references to objects:**

  You can create references to objects using the '&' operator, which is placed in front of a variable. This indicates that the variable is a reference to the object, rather than a separate copy of the object.

```
class MyClass {
    public $property;

    public function __construct($value) {
        $this->property = $value;
    }
}

$obj1 = new MyClass("Object 1");
$refObj = $obj1; // Creating a reference to $obj1

$refObj->property = "Updated from reference";
echo $obj1->property; // Output: "Updated from reference"
```

In this example, both **$obj1** and **$refObj** point to the same object, so when you modify the object using one of them, the change is reflected in the other.

Conclusion

This chapter has provided a comprehensive overview of OOP in PHP, covering a wide range of essential topics. We have explored the fundamental concepts of creating classes and objects, defining properties and methods, and understanding access specifiers. The principles of encapsulation, the '$this' variable, and the usage of constructors and destructors have been thoroughly explained. Additionally, we have delved into more advanced OOP techniques, including overloading, overriding, abstract classes, polymorphism, and interfaces, while also discussing the significance of the 'final' keyword and references. Armed with this knowledge, you are now well-prepared to harness the power of OOP in PHP, allowing you to create more structured and flexible code for your web applications.

In the next chapter we will explore PHP security, and safeguarding applications built with the popular server-side scripting language PHP from a range of potential threats and vulnerabilities.

Points to remember

- **Object-oriented basics**: Understand the fundamental principles of OOP, which include classes, objects, properties, and methods.
- **Access specifiers**: Learn how access specifiers like public, private, and protected control the visibility and access of class members.
- **Encapsulation**: Recognize the importance of encapsulation in OOP, which involves bundling data (properties) and methods that operate on that data within a class to protect it.
- **Constructors and destructors**: Constructors are special methods that initialize objects, while destructors are used for cleanup. Remember how to use them effectively.
- **Method overloading and overriding**: Understand the concepts of method overloading (having multiple methods with the same name but different parameters) and method overriding (redefining a method in a subclass).
- **Abstract classes**: Abstract classes cannot be instantiated and are meant to be extended by other classes. Remember when and how to use them.
- **Polymorphism**: Grasp the concept of polymorphism, where objects of different classes can be treated as objects of a common base class. This allows for more flexible and extensible code.
- **Interfaces**: Interfaces define a contract that implementing classes must adhere to. Remember how to declare and implement interfaces in your code.

- **Final keyword**: Understand how the 'final' keyword is used to restrict the further extension of a class or method, making it immutable.
- **References**: Learn how to work with references in PHP, which allows multiple variables to refer to the same data in memory.

Join our book's Discord space

Join the book's Discord Workspace for Latest updates, Offers, Tech happenings around the world, New Release and Sessions with the Authors:

https://discord.bpbonline.com

CHAPTER 10
PHP Security

Introduction

PHP security is an essential aspect of web development, focusing on safeguarding applications built with the popular server-side scripting language PHP from a range of potential threats and vulnerabilities. As PHP is commonly used in web applications accessible over the internet, it becomes susceptible to security risks like SQL injection, **Cross-Site Scripting (XSS)**, and more.

To ensure the integrity and confidentiality of data, PHP developers must employ practices such as input validation, output escaping, secure database access, and robust session management. Additionally, maintaining updated software, conducting security testing, and configuring proper error handling are vital steps in fortifying PHP applications against potential breaches and malicious attacks.

Structure

In this chapter, we will cover the following topics:

- Common security threats
- Securing your PHP code
- Protecting against SQL injection attacks

- User authentication and authorization

Objectives

The objective of this chapter is to provide a comprehensive understanding of PHP security and best practices for safeguarding web applications. It begins by addressing common security threats prevalent in PHP applications raising awareness of potential vulnerabilities.

The chapter then delves into strategies for securing PHP code, emphasizing practices like input validation, output escaping, and secure database access. It explores the critical topic of protecting against SQL injection attacks, offering guidance on using prepared statements and input validation to prevent this pervasive threat. Finally, the chapter discusses user authentication and authorization, elucidating the processes by which users are verified and granted appropriate access, ensuring a holistic and robust approach to PHP security. By the end of this chapter, readers will be equipped with the knowledge and techniques required to develop secure and resilient PHP applications in the face of potential security risks.

Common security threats

PHP is a popular server-side scripting language, and like any other web development technology, it is susceptible to various security threats. Common security threats in PHP applications include:

- **SQL Injection (SQLi)**: This occurs when user input is not properly sanitized before being used in database queries. Attackers can inject malicious SQL code, potentially leading to unauthorized access to the database or data leakage.

- **Cross-Site Scripting**: XSS vulnerabilities occur when user-generated content is not properly sanitized and is rendered in a web page without escaping HTML or JavaScript. Attackers can inject scripts that run in the context of other users' browsers, potentially stealing sensitive data or executing actions on behalf of users.

- **Cross-Site Request Forgery (CSRF)**: CSRF attacks trick users into performing actions without their consent when they are logged into a web application. Attackers can forge requests that appear legitimate, causing users to change settings or make unwanted transactions inadvertently.

- **File inclusion vulnerabilities**: Poorly secured file inclusion functions can allow attackers to include malicious files from external sources. This can lead to the execution of arbitrary code on the server, potentially compromising the entire application.

- **Code injection**: Attackers can inject malicious code (for example, PHP code) into user inputs, potentially gaining unauthorized access or executing arbitrary code on the server.

- **Session hijacking and fixation**: Weak or predictable session management can allow attackers to hijack user sessions or set their own session IDs, potentially gaining unauthorized access to user accounts.
- **Insecure file uploads**: If file upload functionality is not properly secured, attackers can upload malicious files that can be executed on the server, leading to various security risks.
- **Insecure authentication**: Weak password policies, storing passwords in plaintext, and insufficient account lockout mechanisms can make it easier for attackers to gain unauthorized access to user accounts.
- **Information disclosure**: Poor error handling and configuration settings can expose sensitive information about the server, database, or application, providing attackers with valuable information for further attacks.
- **Insecure dependencies**: Using outdated or vulnerable third-party libraries or components can introduce security risks. It is essential to keep dependencies up-to-date and apply security patches.
- **Data exposure**: Exposing sensitive data, such as API keys, database credentials, or encryption keys, in the source code or configuration files can lead to data breaches if an attacker gains access to them.
- **Insecure deserialization**: Untrusted data should not be deserialized without proper validation. Insecure deserialization can lead to remote code execution.
- **Lack of input validation**: Failing to validate user input can allow attackers to provide unexpected or malicious data, leading to various vulnerabilities.

To mitigate these security threats in PHP applications, developers should follow best practices like input validation; output escaping, using prepared statements for database queries, implementing secure session management, and keeping the PHP environment and third-party dependencies up-to-date. Additionally, **Web Application Firewalls (WAFs)** and security testing, such as penetration testing and code reviews, can help identify and address security vulnerabilities.

Mitigating vulnerabilities

Mitigating and fixing vulnerabilities in PHP requires a combination of secure coding practices, regular software updates, and continuous monitoring. Here are ways to fix or mitigate vulnerabilities in PHP:

- **Update PHP and dependencies:**
    - Keep PHP and its associated libraries and extensions up to date. Regularly update to the latest stable versions to patch known vulnerabilities.

- Keep track of the dependencies your PHP project relies on, including frameworks, libraries, and packages. Regularly check for updates and apply them to address vulnerabilities in these components.
- Conduct regular penetration testing on your PHP application to identify and address any potential security weaknesses.

- **Secure coding practices:**
  - Use secure coding practices to prevent common vulnerabilities, such as input validation and output encoding.
  - Avoid using **`eval()`** and other functions that execute arbitrary code.
  - Implement least privilege principles by ensuring that code and processes have only the necessary permissions.

- **Input validation and sanitization:**
  - Validate and sanitize all user inputs to prevent SQL injection, XSS, and other injection attacks.
  - Use filtering and validation functions like **`filter_var()`** to ensure that data meets the expected format.

- **Use prepared statements and parameterized queries:**
  - Whenever interacting with a database, use prepared statements or parameterized queries to prevent SQL injection.
  - When dealing with user input in web requests, use parameterized queries to prevent common vulnerabilities like XSS.

- **Implement output encoding:**
  - Encode user-generated content and data before displaying it in web pages to prevent XSS attacks.
  - Use functions like **`htmlspecialchars()`** or frameworks that automatically encode output.

- **CSRF protection:**
  - Implement anti-CSRF tokens to ensure that requests originate from trusted sources.
  - Validate and verify request tokens for each critical action.

- **File inclusion prevention:**
  - Avoid dynamic file inclusion based on user input.
  - Use whitelisting to specify which files can be included and validate file paths.

- **Secure file and directory permissions:**
  - Limit file and directory permissions to the minimum required for your PHP application.
  - Regularly review and set appropriate permissions for sensitive files.
- **Secure session management:**
  - Use strong and unique session IDs.
  - Store sessions securely and configure session parameters for security (e.g., HTTP-only and secure flags on cookies).
  - Implement session timeouts and regenerate session IDs upon login.
- **Security headers:**
  - Set security headers in your application, such as **Content Security Policy** (**CSP**), X-Content-Type-Options, X-Frame-Options, and X-XSS-Protection, to mitigate various attacks.
  - Enable **HTTP Strict Transport Security** (**HSTS**) headers to ensure that communication between the browser and your server occurs over a secure, encrypted connection (HTTPS).
- **Secure authentication and authorization:**
  - Use strong password policies and encourage users to use complex passwords.
  - Implement proper authentication mechanisms, such as password hashing (for example, bcrypt) and **Multi-Factor Authentication** (**MFA**).
- **Intrusion detection and prevention:**
  - Implement **Intrusion Detection** Systems (**IDS**) and **Intrusion Prevention Systems** (**IPS**) to monitor and block suspicious activities.
  - Deploy a **Web** Application **Firewall** (**WAF**) to detect and prevent common web application attacks, such as SQL injection, **Cross-Site Scripting** (**XSS**), and **Cross-Site Request Forgery** (**CSRF**).
- **Regular security audits and penetration testing:**
  - Conduct regular security audits and penetration testing to identify and fix vulnerabilities.
  - Address any findings promptly and implement necessary security improvements.
- **Web Application Firewall (WAF):**
  - Consider using a Web Application Firewall to filter and monitor incoming traffic for potential threats and attacks.

    - Leverage the WAF to block known malicious patterns and signatures associated with common attacks. Subscribe to threat intelligence feeds and regularly update the WAF rule sets to stay current with emerging threats.

- **Stay informed:**
    - Keep abreast of the latest security threats, vulnerabilities, and best practices in PHP and web application security.
    - Subscribe to security mailing lists and follow security news sources.

- **Code review:**
    - Perform regular code reviews with a focus on security.
    - Use static analysis tools to scan code for vulnerabilities.

- **Logging and monitoring:**
    - Implement logging and monitoring to detect and respond to security incidents.
    - Monitor access logs, error logs, and application behavior for suspicious activity.

By following these practices and staying vigilant, you can significantly reduce the risk of vulnerabilities in your PHP applications and enhance their security. It's important to approach security as an ongoing process and not just a one-time fix.

Securing your PHP code

Securing your PHP code is crucial to protect your applications and data from potential threats and vulnerabilities. Here are some essential ways to enhance the security of your PHP code:

- **Input validation:**
    - Always validate and sanitize user inputs to prevent common vulnerabilities like SQL injection and XSS.
    - Use functions like `filter_input` and regular expressions to validate data.

- **Output escaping:**
    - Escape output data when displaying it in HTML or other contexts to prevent XSS attacks. PHP offers functions like **htmlspecialchars** for this purpose.
    - If using a template engine to separate PHP logic from HTML presentation, ensure that the engine supports automatic output escaping. Many modern PHP template engines, such as Twig, automatically escape variables by default.

- **Secure database access:**
  - Use prepared statements and parameterized queries when interacting with databases to prevent SQL injection.
  - Avoid using root or highly privileged database accounts in your application.
- **Session management:**
  - Ensure secure session handling by configuring session settings correctly, using secure cookies, and regenerating session IDs after login.
  - Store session data securely and avoid storing sensitive information in session variables.
- **File handling security:**
  - Validate file uploads rigorously, including checking file types and limiting file permissions.
  - Avoid using user input directly in file paths to prevent directory traversal attacks.
- **Authentication and authorization:**
  - Implement strong authentication mechanisms, such as password hashing with salts, and use secure storage for user credentials.
  - Enforce access control policies to restrict access to specific resources and functionalities.
- **Error handling:**
  - Customize error messages and disable detailed error information in the production environment to prevent exposing sensitive data about your application.
  - Implement custom error handling functions to control how errors are handled and displayed in a production environment.
- **Secure configuration:**
  - Protect configuration files that contain sensitive information like database credentials and encryption keys. Use file permissions to restrict access.
  - Avoid storing sensitive information, such as database credentials and API keys, directly in your PHP code. Instead, store these values in configuration files outside the webroot and include them in your PHP scripts.
- **Regular updates:**
  - Keep PHP, libraries, and dependencies up to date to benefit from security patches and updates.

    - Regularly update your PHP installation to the latest stable version provided by the official PHP website.

- **Security testing:**
    - Conduct security testing, such as penetration testing and code reviews, to identify and address vulnerabilities.
    - Consider using WAFs to add an additional layer of security.

- **Logging and monitoring:**
    - Implement comprehensive logging to track and monitor application activities, assisting in identifying suspicious activities and incident response
    - Establish a security event monitoring system to actively monitor logs for signs of suspicious activity or security incidents.

- **CSRF protection:**
    - Implement anti-CSRF tokens in forms to prevent CSRF attacks.
    - Set the **SameSite** attribute for cookies to mitigate CSRF attacks that exploit the user's browser to perform unauthorized actions on behalf of the user.

- **Use secure file storage:**
    - Store sensitive data securely, and avoid storing sensitive information, such as passwords, in plaintext in your code or configuration files.
    - Place these files in a directory that is not accessible via HTTP requests. This prevents accidental exposure of sensitive information if there are misconfigurations or security vulnerabilities in the web server.

- **Educate developers:**
    - Train your development team about security best practices to ensure that everyone involved in the project understands their role in maintaining security.
    - Encourage developers to stay up to date with security-related news, publications, and industry trends.

- **Stay informed:**
    - Keep up-to-date with the latest security threats and best practices by following security blogs, forums, and industry news.
    - Set up notifications for security mailing lists and regularly check authoritative security databases to stay current with the latest vulnerabilities and recommended mitigations.

By incorporating these security measures into your PHP code development and consistently following best practices, you can significantly reduce the risk of security vulnerabilities and create a more robust and secure application.

Protecting against SQL injection attacks

Protecting against SQL injection attacks is crucial to safeguard your PHP applications and databases. SQL injection is a type of security vulnerability where attackers can manipulate SQL queries by injecting malicious SQL code into user inputs. Here are important measures to protect your PHP code from SQL injection:

- **Use prepared statements and parameterized queries:**

  Instead of directly embedding user inputs into SQL queries, use prepared statements provided by PDO or MySQLi. These statements separate SQL code from user inputs, preventing SQL injection.

  Example using PDO:

  ```
  $stmt = $pdo->prepare("SELECT * FROM users WHERE username = :username");
  $stmt->execute(['username' => $userInput]);
  ```

  ```
  Example using MySQLi:
  $stmt = $mysqli->prepare("SELECT * FROM users WHERE username = ?");
  $stmt->bind_param("s", $userInput); $stmt->execute();
  ```

- **Input validation and sanitization:**

  Validate and sanitize user inputs to ensure that they meet expected criteria. While input validation is essential, it should be used in conjunction with prepared statements for complete protection.

- **Avoid dynamic SQL queries:**

  Avoid constructing SQL queries dynamically by concatenating user inputs into the query string. If you must construct dynamic queries, ensure that you're using prepared statements and that user inputs are properly sanitized.

- **Limit database user privileges:**

  Use the principle of least privilege for your database users. Restrict the permissions of the user account used by your PHP application to only those necessary for its functions.

- **Database escape functions:**

  If you cannot use prepared statements, use database-specific escape functions like **`mysqli_real_escape_string`** or **`PDO::quote`** to escape user inputs before embedding them in SQL queries. While this is less secure than prepared statements, direct insertion is still better.

Example using `mysqli_real_escape_string`:

```
$userInput = mysqli_real_escape_string($conn, $userInput);

$query = "SELECT * FROM users WHERE username = '$userInput'";
```

Stored procedures:

Consider using stored procedures as an extra layer of defense. They can encapsulate SQL logic within the database, reducing the risk of SQL injection.

- **Input data validation:**

  Ensure that input data adheres to expected data types, lengths, and formats. Reject any inputs that don't meet these criteria.

- **Content Security Policy:**

  Implement a content security policy that restricts the sources from which external content (such as scripts) can be loaded on your web page. This helps protect against XSS attacks, which can be used to execute SQL injection.

- **Regular updates and security patching:**

  Keep your PHP, database server, and associated libraries up to date. Updates often include security patches that address known vulnerabilities.

- **Security testing:**

  Perform security testing, including automated and manual code reviews, to identify and address SQL injection vulnerabilities.

By implementing these measures, you can significantly reduce the risk of SQL injection attacks in your PHP applications and enhance the security of your database interactions.

User authentication and authorization

User authentication and authorization are crucial components of web application security. They ensure that only authorized users can access specific resources or execute certain actions within an application. Here is an overview of both concepts:

- **User authentication:**

  Authentication is the process of verifying the identity of a user. It ensures that a user is who they claim to be. In the context of web applications, user authentication typically involves validating a user's credentials, such as a username and password.

Key points in user authentication:

- **User credentials**: Users provide their credentials, typically a username and password, during the authentication process.
- **Secure storage**: User passwords should be securely stored in the database using techniques like password hashing with salt to prevent exposure in the event of a data breach.
- **Authentication methods**: Consider various authentication methods, such as multi-factor authentication, to enhance security.
- **Session management**: Once a user is authenticated, a session is established to keep the user's identity across multiple requests.

- **User authorization:**

  Authorization is the process of determining what actions and resources a user is allowed to access within an application after authentication. It ensures that users only have access to the features and data that they are permitted to use.

  Key points in user authorization:

  - **Access control**: Define access control policies that specify which users or groups of users can access specific parts of the application.
  - **Role-Based Access Control (RBAC)**: Implement RBAC to assign users to roles, and grant or deny access based on roles. For example, roles like "admin," "user," and "guest" may have different permissions.
  - **Permissions and privileges**: Specify fine-grained permissions for actions, such as read, write, or delete, for different resources within the application.
  - **API and resource authorization**: Ensure that APIs, database queries, and resource access (for example, files) are also authorized. Restrict API endpoints and database queries based on user permissions.
  - **Dynamic authorization**: Some applications require dynamic or attribute-based authorization, where access is determined based on specific conditions, user attributes, or data content.
  - **Security tokens**: Implement security tokens or access tokens for more secure and stateless authorization, particularly in the context of APIs and microservices.

In practice, authentication and authorization are often closely entwined. Authentication establishes the user's identity, and authorization determines what actions or resources the authenticated user can access. Web application frameworks and libraries, like Laravel, Symfony, and OAuth 2.0, offer built-in tools and mechanisms to help implement both authentication and authorization effectively and securely.

It is decisive to regularly review and update your authentication and authorization mechanisms to adapt to changing security threats and requirements, ultimately maintaining a robust and secure application.

Protecting your PHP web application from cyber-attacks

Protecting your PHP web application from cyber-attacks is pivotal to ensuring the security and integrity of your system. Considering the widespread utilization of PHP in web applications, ensuring security is not a choice but a mandatory requirement. To safeguard your application against PHP vulnerabilities, you should consider implementing the following measures:

- **Keep software up-to-date:** Ensure that your PHP version, web server (for example, Apache, Nginx), and database software are regularly updated to patch security vulnerabilities.

- **Use a WAF:** Implement a WAF to filter and monitor incoming traffic for malicious requests and attacks, providing an additional layer of protection.

- **Validate user input:** Always validate and sanitize user input to prevent SQL injection, XSS, and other injection attacks. Use prepared statements or parameterized queries when interacting with databases.

- **Secure configuration:** Review and configure your PHP application, web server, and database for optimal security settings. Disable unnecessary services, directories, and features.

- **Authentication and authorization:** Implement strong user authentication and authorization mechanisms. Use secure password storage practices like hashing and salting passwords. Implement proper role-based access control.

- **Cross-Site Request Forgery (CSRF) protection:** Protect against CSRF attacks by using anti-CSRF tokens in your forms and checking them on the server.

- **Cross-Origin Resource Sharing (CORS):** Set up appropriate CORS policies to control which domains can access your web application's resources.

- **Content Security Policy:** Implement a CSP to restrict the sources of content that can be executed in your web application, reducing the risk of XSS attacks.

- **Secure file uploads:** If your application allows file uploads, validate file types, limit file size, and store uploaded files in a secure location with restricted access.

- **Secure session management:** Use secure session handling mechanisms, such as session tokens, and ensure sessions are properly destroyed after a user logs out.

- **Error handling:** Avoid exposing sensitive information in error messages to potential attackers. Customize error messages to be informative to developers but not to users.
- **Regular security testing:** Conduct regular security assessments, such as penetration testing, vulnerability scanning, and code reviews, to identify and fix security issues. Implement rate limiting on APIs and login forms to prevent brute-force and DoS attacks.
- **SSL/TLS encryption:** Use SSL / TLS encryption to secure data transmission between your web application and clients. Ensure that your SSL / TLS configurations are up to date and properly configured.
- **Monitor logs and intrusion detection:** Set up log monitoring and intrusion detection systems to detect and respond to security incidents in real-time.
- **Backups:** Regularly backup your application's data and configurations. Ensure backups are stored securely and can be restored in case of a breach.
- **Third-party libraries:** Keep third-party libraries and dependencies updated to patch known vulnerabilities.
- **Security headers:** Set appropriate security headers in your application to protect against various types of attacks, such as clickjacking and XSS.
- **Educate your team:** Train your development and operations teams about security best practices and encourage a security-first mindset.
- **Incident response plan:** Develop and regularly update an incident response plan to handle security breaches effectively and minimize their impact. Remember that security is an ongoing process, and it is important to stay informed about the latest security threats and best practices to protect your PHP web application effectively.

Net solutions to build secure PHP websites

To build secure PHP websites, you should implement a comprehensive security strategy. Begin with vigorous WAFs to filter malicious traffic and enforce security policies. Employ a CSP to alleviate XSS risks. Keep software, including PHP, web servers, and databases, up to date and promptly patch known vulnerabilities. Focus on secure coding practices, conduct regular code reviews, and use security headers to protect against various web-based threats.

Implement **Two-Factor Authentication** (**2FA**) for user access and prioritize data encryption in transit and at rest. Logging and monitoring solutions are essential for detecting and responding to security incidents in real time. Regular security audits, penetration testing, and vulnerability scanning help identify and rectify weaknesses. Lastly, create a well-defined incident response plan to manage breaches effectively and reduce their impact.

By combining these measures, you can build and maintain secure PHP websites.Top of Form

Conclusion

This chapter has provided a comprehensive exploration of PHP security, beginning with an examination of common security threats that can influence web applications. We then delved into essential approaches for securing PHP code, highlighting the significance of input validation, output escaping, and secure database access. To combat one of the most prevalent threats, SQL injection, we discussed the importance of using prepared statements and input validation techniques. Finally, we explored user authentication and authorization, crucial components for controlling access and ensuring data integrity.

By understanding these fundamental principles and best practices, you are now well-equipped to build resilient and secure PHP applications that can withstand potential security challenges, safeguarding both your data and your users' online experiences.

The next chapter will deal with PHP best practices and advanced topics. We will unravel strategies for creating clean, maintainable, and scalable PHP codebases.

Points to remember

- Emphasize input validation and output escaping to prevent security vulnerabilities.
- Ensure that user inputs are thoroughly validated and sanitized to protect against potential attacks.
- Use prepared statements and parameterized queries to defend against SQL injection, one of the most prevalent threats.
- Avoid constructing dynamic SQL queries with user inputs unless you're using prepared statements.
- Authentication is the process of verifying user identities, while authorization determines what actions and resources they can access.
- Implement strong authentication mechanisms, such as password hashing, and enforce access control through role-based or attribute-based authorization.
- Use secure cookies and regenerate session IDs to prevent session hijacking.
- Consider scenarios where access control policies depend on dynamic factors or user attributes, and implement dynamic or attribute-based authorization.
- Keep your PHP, databases, and libraries up to date to mitigate vulnerabilities.
- Conduct security testing through code reviews and penetration testing to identify and address security flaws.

Chapter 11
PHP Best Practices and Advanced Topics

Introduction

PHP development will elevate to a more sophisticated level by focusing on code organization and structure. We will unravel strategies for creating clean, maintainable, and scalable PHP codebases. After that, we will tackle the critical skills of debugging and error handling, equipping you with the tools to identify and rectify issues efficiently. The journey continues with a deep dive into performance optimization techniques, ensuring your PHP applications run smoothly and efficiently. We will then navigate the landscape of PHP frameworks, explaining how these powerful tools can enhance development workflows. Lastly, we will explore the integration of APIs and web services, providing you with the knowledge to seamlessly connect your PHP applications with external systems. By the end of this chapter, you will possess a robust understanding of advanced PHP concepts, empowering you to craft high quality, efficient, and well-structured web applications. Let us embark on this journey to elevate your PHP development skills to new heights.

Structure

In this chapter, we will cover the following topics:

- Code organization and structure
- Use modern PHP versions

- Advanced Topics
- Debugging and error handling
- Performance optimization
- Using PHP frameworks
- APIs and web services
- Adopting WebSockets
- Leverage asynchronous programming

Objectives

This chapter aims to equip readers with an in-depth understanding of sophisticated PHP development techniques, emphasizing code organization, use of modern PHP versions debugging, and error handling. Readers will dig into the details of optimizing PHP code for enhanced performance, exploring advanced topics such as leveraging PHP frameworks to streamline development processes. The chapter also covers the integration of APIs and web services, providing insights into best practices for seamless communication between applications. By the end of this chapter, readers should have a comprehensive grasp of advanced PHP concepts, enabling them to develop well-organized, efficient, and robust applications in accordance with industry best practices.

Code organization and structure

Code organization and structure in PHP are fundamental aspects of building maintainable, scalable, and readable applications. Adhering to best practices in code organization is crucial for collaboration among developers and for the long-term sustainability of a project. Here are some recommended practices for code organization and structure in PHP:

- **Directory structure:**

  Organize your project files into logical directories such as src for source code, public for publicly accessible files, tests for unit tests, and so on.

- **Namespace and auto-loading:**

  Use namespaces to avoid naming conflicts and make your code more modular. Set up an autoloader to automatically load classes without the need for manual includes.

  ```
  // Example of namespace and autoloading
  namespace MyApp;
  spl_autoload_register(function ($class) {
      include 'src/' . str_replace('\\', '/', $class) . '.php';
  });
  ```

- **PSR standards:**

  Follow the **PHP Standard Recommendations (PSR)** standards, such as PSR-1, PSR-2, and PSR-4, to maintain consistency across your codebase and make it more interoperable with other PHP projects.

- **Separation of concerns:**

  Adhere to the principle of separation of concerns by dividing your code into different layers, such as separating business logic from presentation logic. Use a framework or design pattern (for example, MVC) to achieve this.

- **Use classes and objects:**

  Encapsulate functionality into classes and objects. This promotes reusability, maintainability, and makes your code more object-oriented.

```
// Example of a class in PHP
class MyClass {
    private $property;
    public function __construct($value) {
        $this->property = $value;
    }
    public function getProperty() {
        return $this->property;
    }
}
```

- **Configuration management:**

  Separate configuration settings from code. Store configuration parameters in external files (for example, .env files) and use a configuration manager to access them.

- **Documentation:**

  Document your code using comments and/or external documentation tools. This makes it easier for developers to understand your code and contributes to the overall maintainability.

```
// Example of code documentation
/**
 * This function does something.
 *
 * @param string $param1 Description of the parameter
```

```
 * @return int Description of the return value
 */
function myFunction($param1) {
    // function implementation
}
```

- **Error handling:**

  Implement robust error-handling mechanisms to gracefully handle errors and exceptions. Log errors for debugging purposes and present user-friendly error messages.

  ```
  // Example of error handling
  try {
      // code that may throw an exception
  } catch (Exception $e) {
      // handle the exception
      error_log('Caught exception: ' . $e->getMessage());
  }
  ```

By following these practices, you can create well-organized, maintainable, and scalable PHP applications that are easier to develop, debug, and extend over time.

Use modern PHP versions

Using modern PHP versions is considered a best practice in PHP development for several reasons, encompassing performance improvements, security enhancements, and access to new language features. Let's explore these aspects and some advanced topics related to modern PHP development.

Performance improvements:

- **OpCode caching:** Modern PHP versions come with improved opcode caching mechanisms, such as OPCache, which significantly boosts performance by storing precompiled script bytecode in memory.
- **JIT compilation:** Some PHP versions introduce Just-In-Time compilation, further optimizing the execution of PHP code.

Security enhancements:

- **Security patches:** Using the latest PHP versions ensures that your application benefits from the latest security patches, addressing vulnerabilities and minimizing the risk of exploitation.

- **Secure defaults:** Modern PHP versions often come with more secure default configurations, reducing the likelihood of misconfigurations leading to security issues.

Language features:

- **Scalar type declarations:** PHP 7 introduced scalar type declarations, allowing developers to define the expected data type for function parameters and return values.
- **Return type declarations:** Similarly, PHP 7 added return type declarations, enabling developers to specify the expected return type of a function.
- **Nullable types:** In later PHP versions, nullable types were introduced, allowing developers to indicate that a variable can be of a certain type or **null**.
- **Arrow functions:** PHP 7.4 introduced arrow functions, providing a more concise syntax for anonymous functions.
- **Attributes (Annotations):** PHP 8 introduced attributes, enabling developers to add metadata to classes, methods, and properties.

Error handling:

- **Throwable Interface:** Modern PHP versions allow catching exceptions and errors using the **Throwable** interface, offering a unified way to handle both exceptions and errors.

Advanced topics

Some advanced topics about PHP are as follows:

- **Dependency management:** Embrace **Composer** for package management. Define and manage project dependencies efficiently using Composer.
- **Containerization:** Containerization using **Docker** facilitates consistent environments across different development stages and deployments.
- **Testing:** Adopt **PHPUnit** for unit testing. Write comprehensive test suites to ensure the reliability and correctness of your code.
- **Framework utilization:** Leverage popular PHP frameworks like **Symfony, Laravel, etc.** for structured development, built-in features, and community support.
- **Database abstraction:** Explore ORM **(Object-Relational Mapping)** libraries like Doctrine for efficient database interactions and abstraction.
- **Continuous Integration/Continuous Deployment (CI/CD):** Implement CI/CD pipelines to automate testing, deployment, and ensure a streamlined development process example **GitLab CI, GitHub Actions, etc.**.

- **Security practices:** Follow the **OWASP guidelines** for secure coding practices. Implement input validation, secure session management, and protect against common web vulnerabilities.

- **Performance optimization:** Implement **caching mechanisms** for frequently used data. Consider using tools like Redis or Memcached for caching.

- **Asynchronous PHP:** Explore asynchronous PHP frameworks/libraries like **Swoole, ReactPHP** for building high-performance, non-blocking applications.

- **Logging and monitoring:** Implement robust logging and monitoring solutions like **Monolog, New Relic, etc.** to track application behavior and performance.

Staying up-to-date with modern PHP versions and adopting best practices and advanced topics in PHP development contributes to code quality, security, and overall application performance.

Debugging and error handling

Debugging and error handling are critical components of PHP development, and they play a crucial role in optimizing code for performance and reliability. It will be helpful to ensure smooth execution, identify issues, and provide meaningful feedback for both developers and users. Below are some best practices for debugging and error handling in PHP:

- **Debugging:** Debugging in PHP involves identifying and fixing errors or issues in your code to ensure it runs correctly.

  Use var_dump and print_r:

  These functions are invaluable for inspecting variables and data structures during development. They provide detailed information about the type and value of a variable.

  ```
  $data = [1, 2, 3];
  var_dump($data);
  ```

- **Logging:** Implement logging using functions like **`error_log`** or a dedicated logging library. Logging allows you to record information about the application's behavior, making it easier to identify issues.

  ```
  // Example logging
  error_log('An error occurred: Something went wrong.');
  ```

- **Use echo and die statements:** While not suitable for production, strategically placing echo or die statements in your code can help identify where issues might be occurring.

  ```
  echo 'Debugging point reached.';
  ```

- **Xdebug and profilers**: Utilize Xdebug or other profilers to profile your code and identify performance bottlenecks. Xdebug can generate detailed reports on function calls, memory usage, and execution time.
- **Error handling:** Error handling in PHP is crucial for identifying and resolving issues that may occur during the execution of a script. PHP provides several techniques for error handling, including try-catch block, built-in error reporting functions, custom error handlers, and exceptions.
- **Try-catch blocks:** Use try-catch blocks to handle exceptions gracefully. This prevents fatal errors from terminating the script and allows you to handle errors in a controlled manner.

```
try {
    // code that may throw an exception
} catch (Exception $e) {
    // handle the exception
    echo 'Caught exception: ', $e->getMessage();
}
```

- **Custom error handling functions:** Implement custom error handling functions using **set_error_handler** to capture PHP errors and handle them according to your application's needs.

```
function customErrorHandler($errno, $errstr, $errfile, $errline) {
    // handle the error
}
set_error_handler('customErrorHandler');
```

- **Use error_reporting wisely:** Adjust the error reporting level based on the development stage. In production, set it to a lower level to prevent sensitive information from being exposed.

```
// In development
error_reporting(E ALL);
ini_set('display_errors', 1);
// In production
error_reporting(E_ERROR | E_PARSE);
ini_set('display_errors', 0);
```

- **Graceful degradation:** Implement graceful degradation by providing fallback mechanisms when certain functionality is unavailable. This ensures that users experience a smooth transition even when errors occur.

- **Handle expected errors**: Anticipate and handle expected errors, such as file not found or database connection issues. Implement appropriate fallbacks or user-friendly error messages.

```
if (!file_exists('myfile.txt')) {
    // handle file not found error
}
```

By incorporating these debugging and error-handling practices into your PHP code, you can streamline the development process, identify and fix issues efficiently, and create more robust and optimized applications.

Performance optimization

Performance optimization is crucial in PHP development to ensure that web applications run efficiently and respond quickly to user requests. Here are some key strategies for optimizing the performance of PHP code:

- **Use OpCode caching:** OpCode caching tools, such as OPcache, store compiled PHP code in memory, reducing the need for recompilation on every request. This significantly improves the execution speed of PHP scripts.
- **Database optimization:** Optimize database queries by using indexes, retrieving only the necessary data, and caching frequently used queries. Consider denormalizing data when appropriate and using database connection pooling.
- **Minimize HTTP requests:** Reduce the number of HTTP requests by combining CSS and JavaScript files, using image sprites, and utilizing asynchronous loading techniques. This minimizes the time it takes for a browser to fetch resources.
- **Optimize code execution:** Write efficient and optimized code by avoiding unnecessary loops, minimizing function calls, and using built-in functions for common tasks. Profile your code to identify bottlenecks and optimize accordingly.
- **Caching strategies:** Implement caching mechanisms for frequently accessed data. Use techniques such as object caching, page caching, and full-page caching to reduce the load on the server.
- **Use a Content Delivery Network (CDN):** Distribute static assets, such as images, stylesheets, and scripts, across a network of servers globally. This reduces latency and accelerates the delivery of content to users.
- **Enable Gzip compression:** Enable Gzip compression to reduce the size of data sent between the server and the client. This significantly speeds up the loading time of web pages.
- **Lazy loading:** Implement lazy loading for resources such as images and scripts. Load content only when it is needed, reducing the initial page load time.

- **Optimize autoloading:** Use an efficient autoloader, such as the one provided by Composer. Avoid excessive file inclusion and only load the classes that are required for the current request.
- **Upgrade PHP version:** Ensure that you are using the latest stable version of PHP, as each new version typically includes performance improvements and optimizations.
- **Implement a CDN:** Utilize a CDN to distribute static assets, such as images, stylesheets, and scripts, across multiple servers worldwide. This reduces latency and accelerates content delivery to users.
- **Load balancing:** Implement load balancing across multiple servers to distribute incoming traffic evenly. This helps prevent any single server from becoming a performance bottleneck.
- **Monitor and analyze:** Regularly monitor your application's performance using tools like New Relic, Blackfire, or XHProf. Analyze the results to identify areas for improvement and optimize accordingly.
- **Use efficient algorithms and data structures:** Choose the right algorithms and data structures for your application. Optimize critical sections of code to ensure efficient processing.

By incorporating these performance optimization techniques into your PHP development workflow, you can create web applications that deliver a faster and more responsive user experience.

Using PHP frameworks

Use of PHP frameworks is common in web development to streamline the development process, enforce best practices, and promote code organization. PHP frameworks provide a structured and efficient way to build robust web applications. In the following ways, we can use PHP frameworks effectively:

- **Choose the right framework:** Select a PHP framework based on your project requirements, team expertise, and the features provided by the framework. Popular PHP frameworks include Laravel, Symfony, CodeIgniter, Yii, and Zend.
- **Installation:** Follow the installation instructions provided by the framework's documentation. Most frameworks can be installed via Composer, a dependency manager for PHP.

  ```
  composer create-project laravel/laravel my-project
  ```

- **Directory structure:** Familiarize yourself with the directory structure imposed by the framework. Understand the purpose of each directory, such as app, config, public, and resources.

- **Configuration:** Configure your application settings in the framework's configuration files. This includes database connections, caching, session management, and other environment-specific settings.
- **Routing:** Learn and use the framework's routing system to define the URLs and map them to controllers and actions. Routing helps in creating clean and SEO-friendly URLs for your application.
- **Controllers and views:** Understand how controllers handle incoming requests, process data, and interact with models. Learn how to use views to present data to the user. Most frameworks follow the **Model-View-Controller** (**MVC**) pattern.
- **Database integration:** Explore the framework's database abstraction layer to interact with databases. Familiarize yourself with techniques such as **Object-Relational Mapping** (**ORM**) for simplified database operations.
- **Middleware:** Learn about middleware and how it can be used for tasks like authentication, logging, and modifying the HTTP request and response.
- **Authentication and authorization:** Utilize the built-in features for user authentication and authorization provided by the framework. This includes handling user sessions, passwords, and roles.
- **Dependency injection and IoC:** Understand and leverage dependency injection and **Inversion of Control** (**IoC**) containers provided by the framework. This promotes modular and testable code.
- **Testing:** Explore the framework's testing capabilities. Write unit tests and functional tests to ensure the reliability and correctness of your application.
- **Security best practices:** Adhere to security best practices provided by the framework. This includes input validation, output escaping, and protection against common vulnerabilities like SQL injection and cross-site scripting.
- **Community and documentation:** Join the framework's community forums or chat groups to seek help and share experiences. Refer to the official documentation for detailed information on features, best practices, and updates.
- **Keep up with updates:** Regularly update your framework to the latest version to benefit from bug fixes, security patches, and new features.

Using PHP frameworks can significantly speed up development and improve the maintainability of your code. By understanding the framework's features and best practices, you can harness the full potential of these tools in building modern and efficient web applications.

APIs and web services

Application Programming Interfaces (APIs) and web services play a crucial role in modern web development, allowing different software systems to communicate and interact with each other. Below are some points to understanding APIs and web services:

API

An API is a set of rules and protocols that allows one software application to interact with another. It defines how different software components should communicate, enabling the exchange of data and functionality.

Types of APIs:

- **Web APIs (HTTP APIs)**: These APIs are accessed over the HTTP protocol and are commonly used for web services. RESTful and SOAP are popular web API architectures.
- **Library or framework APIs**: These are APIs provided by programming languages, libraries, or frameworks to simplify development tasks. Examples include the jQuery library in JavaScript or the Django framework in Python.
- **Operating system APIs**: These APIs provide a set of functions and procedures for interacting with the underlying operating system, for example, the Windows API.

Web services

Web services are a specific type of API that is accessible over the web. They facilitate communication and data exchange between different systems over a network, typically using standard web protocols such as HTTP.

Types of web services:

- **RESTful web services**: Based on **Representational State Transfer (REST)** architecture. Utilizes standard HTTP methods (GET, POST, PUT, DELETE) and is often used with JSON as the data format.
- **SOAP web services**: Based on XML and typically uses the XML-based protocol for communication. SOAP provides a standardized way of communication between different applications.

Key concepts in APIs and web services:

- **Endpoints**: URLs or **Uniform Resource Identifiers (URIs)** that indicate where the API or web service can be accessed.
- **HTTP methods**: Standard methods used in HTTP requests, such as GET (retrieve data), POST (submit data), PUT (update data), and DELETE (remove data).

- **Request and response**: Communication between clients and servers involves requests (sent by clients) and responses (sent by servers).

Authentication and authorization:

- **Authentication**: The process of verifying the identity of a user, application, or system accessing the API. Common methods include API keys, OAuth, and JWT.
- **Authorization**: Determines the level of access granted to a user or application. Ensures that users or applications can only access the resources they are allowed to.

RESTful principles:

RESTful APIs adhere to certain principles:

- **Statelessness**: Each request from a client contains all the information needed for the server to fulfill the request. The server does not store information about the client's state between requests.
- **Resource-based**: Resources (data or services) are identified by URIs, and interactions are performed using standard HTTP methods.
- **Representation**: Resources can have multiple representations (e.g., JSON or XML), and clients can negotiate the representation they prefer.

Documentation:

API Documentation: Clearly documented APIs are essential for developers to understand how to use the API, what endpoints are available, required parameters, and expected responses.

Testing and debugging:

- **API Testing**: Tools such as Postman or cURL are commonly used for testing APIs. Ensure that endpoints work as expected, handle errors appropriately, and return the correct data.
- **Debugging**: Use debugging tools provided by the API or third-party tools to troubleshoot issues in API requests and responses.

Best practices:

- **Versioning**: Include version numbers in your API to handle changes gracefully and avoid breaking existing integrations.
- **Rate Limiting**: Implement rate limiting to prevent abuse and ensure fair usage of your API.
- **Security**: Use secure connections (HTTPS), encrypt sensitive data, and validate and sanitize inputs to prevent common security vulnerabilities.

Understanding APIs and web services is essential for modern web development. Whether you are consuming APIs in your applications or creating your own API for others to use, a solid understanding of these concepts will enable seamless integration and communication between different software systems.

Adopting WebSockets

WebSockets represent an advanced and powerful communication protocol that facilitates real-time, bidirectional interaction between web clients and servers. In PHP development, adopting WebSockets involves moving beyond the traditional request-response model, allowing for instant data exchange between clients and servers.

Best practices for implementing WebSockets in PHP include utilizing dedicated WebSocket libraries or frameworks like Ratchet or integrating native solutions such as Swoole. When working with WebSockets, developers should prioritize considerations such as managing concurrent connections, implementing proper security measures, and ensuring scalability to accommodate the potential increase in simultaneous users.

This advanced topic is particularly valuable for applications that demand low-latency updates and real-time collaboration, such as live chat applications, online gaming platforms, or collaborative document editing tools. The incorporation of WebSockets in PHP reflects a commitment to delivering dynamic and interactive user experiences while adhering to best practices in terms of security, scalability, and efficient resource management.

Leverage asynchronous programming

Asynchronous programming in PHP introduces a paradigm shift from traditional synchronous request-response operations, allowing for more efficient handling of concurrent tasks and improved responsiveness in web applications.

As a best practice, developers can leverage asynchronous programming to optimize resource utilization, enhance scalability, and reduce latency. Advanced topics in asynchronous PHP often involve the use of libraries or extensions like ReactPHP or Amp, which provide tools for asynchronous event-driven programming. Key aspects of asynchronous programming include non-blocking I/O operations, allowing PHP to perform other tasks while waiting for data, and the use of Promises or Coroutines to manage asynchronous workflows.

When implementing asynchronous programming in PHP, it's crucial to consider error handling, proper resource management, and potential race conditions. This advanced approach is particularly beneficial for tasks such as handling multiple concurrent requests, interacting with external APIs, or building high-performance web applications where responsiveness is critical. Adopting best practices in asynchronous programming enables PHP developers to create more scalable and efficient systems, enhancing the overall performance of their applications.

Conclusion

This chapter has explored into essential PHP best practices and advanced topics, providing a complete walkthrough for developers to enhance their skills and build robust applications. We explored the critical aspects of code organization and structure, emphasizing the significance of maintaining clean, modular, and scalable codebases. The chapter addressed the complexities of debugging and error handling, offering insights into effective troubleshooting strategies and ensuring the reliability of PHP applications. Additionally, we steered the territory of performance optimization, uncovering techniques to boost the speed and efficiency of PHP code. The exploration of PHP frameworks showcased the power of leveraging structured frameworks like Laravel or Symfony, streamlining development processes, and promoting code reusability. Lastly, a detailed overview of APIs and web services enlightened readers on the principles of seamless communication between software systems, a crucial skill in the contemporary web development landscape. By understanding these advanced topics and following best practices, developers are well-equipped to uplift their PHP proficiency and contribute to the creation of high-quality, efficient, and maintainable web applications.

Points to remember

- **Strategic debugging**: Use tools like var_dump and logging to strategically debug code during development.
- **Try-catch blocks**: Implement try-catch blocks for graceful error handling and preventing fatal crashes.
- **Database optimization**: Optimize database queries through indexing, efficient retrieval, and caching.
- **Efficient code execution**: Write optimized code by avoiding unnecessary loops and function calls.
- **Choose wisely**: Select a PHP framework based on project requirements and team expertise.
- **API types**: Understand different API types, including RESTful and SOAP, and when to use each.
- **HTTP methods**: Understand the significance of HTTP methods like GET, POST, PUT, and DELETE.
- **Testing and debugging**: Utilize tools like Postman for testing APIs and debugging.

Index

X